MAKING THE BEST OF THINGS
LIFE DURING THE WAR YEARS

By

The Women's Research Group

The Women's Research Group has been working to record the lives of women in Coventry since it was established in 1998. It is important that the history of women in the city should not be forgotten. The war years were a particularly memorable time for everyone who lived through it, whatever age, they have a story to tell.

Previous books published by the Women's Research Group:

> Redressing the Balance
> Hurdy Gurdy Days
> Keeping the Balance
> Telling Tales
> All in a Day's Work

ISBN 978-0-9540604-4-2

Acknowledgements

The Women's Research Group would like to thank the following organisations and individuals for their help in preparing this book.

The staff at Local Studies, Central Library, Coventry, for their assistance in research.

Coventry Record Office, Canal Basin, Coventry.

Individuals who have supplied information and photographs of themselves or relatives.

Vic Terry for permission to use the photograph of the VE day party.

CONTENTS

Can You Remember This?

Clothing coupons came into being in 1941. The mark CC41 represented Civilian Clothing and the figure 41 represented the year it was established. The CC41 mark also applied to furniture. The government stated that clothes should use the minimum amount of material and the furniture to be made plain, so as to conserve wood. Today utility furniture has become very collectable.

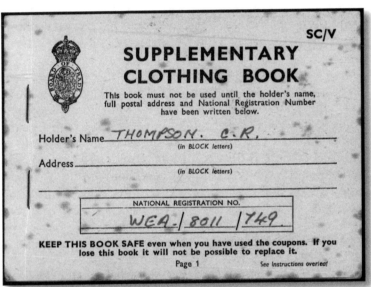

When clothing coupons first came into force the allowance was 66 coupons. In 1942 it was lowered to 60 and in 1943 to 40, however, in 1944 it was increased to 48. When you think that a man's suit used up 26 coupons, a blouse five and a ladies woollen dress 14 coupons, there were not many left for any other items of clothing. Women in factories wore men's socks under their trousers, as they could not afford two coupons for a pair of Rayon stockings. Nylon had not been invented at this time of course; it would have been more durable. Women would paint their legs with gravy browning and draw a black line, with an eyebrow pencil, up the back for a seam. Ladies had French or cami-knickers and underwear was sometimes made out of parachute silk. Parachute material was used for many items even wedding dresses. If you were getting married or were having a baby you could apply for Supplementary Clothing Coupons this also applied if your home had been bombed out. If you wanted material to make an outfit you had to use your coupons. Blackout material was exempt; so many people made skirts and trimmed them with coloured bias binding or embroidered patterns on them to pretty the garment up.

My mother made a pinafore dress out of my uncle's trousers and a blouse from the back of my father's shirt. It was certainly make do and mend. Imagine having to unpick a knitted garment and when it had been washed having to roll the wool into a ball. The wool would then be used again to make another garment. Perhaps that is why boys wore those horrible fair-isle slipovers, most likely wool left over from other articles, just to use up the wool. We probably thought that the knitted pixie-hoods that girls wore were glamorous, particularly with the big woollen bow tied under your chin!

I can remember as a child queuing with my mother outside a wallpaper shop, I think it was called Schofields, in Corporation Street, Coventry, only to be told that they had sold out. We ended up with a tin of distemper (which you had to mix yourself) and a stippling brush instead. I am sure many of us can remember having our walls stippled, how could you forget?

From 1942 onwards, utility furniture could be purchased by newly married couples and by people who had been bombed out of their homes. A permit issued by the Board of Trade was required. The furniture allowance for a couple was 60 units and 10 units for each child. A metal bedstead would be five units, wardrobe 12 units, kitchen table six units, and an armchair six units. A sideboard with the CC41 mark on it would have cost around £10, it would have been very basic but solid.

There were many dressmaking patterns during this time. Weldon's Fashion, *Practical Wear for War Work* blouses, skirts, jackets, boleros etc. Leach-Way produced patterns such as *Fashion with Economy Frocks* as did Bestway *War Time Renovations, Coats and suits from short lengths* and *Economy Design for Underwear*.

People knitted during the war and Weldon produced a Knitting Series *'New Woollies'* for our sailors, soldiers and airmen. Many people knitted socks for the forces.

Rationing began on the 8th January 1940; this was 18 weeks after the outbreak of the war. The ration per week per person was minimal. No obesity around then! You were entitled to 4 ozs bacon and ham, 2 ozs butter, 2ozs cheese, (sometimes this could be a larger amount), 4 ozs of margarine (I always hated this), 4 ozs of cooking fat, but sometimes the amount would be reduced to 2 ozs. You were allocated 3 pints of milk a week, but sometimes it would be only 2 pints. Dried milk was available, but this was one packet every four weeks. Eight ounces of sugar, a one pound jar of jam every two months and 2 ozs of tea. One egg a week if they were available, but sometimes it was one egg every two weeks. Dried egg, which was imported from America you could have every four weeks (as a child I liked the dried egg better than a fresh egg). Every four weeks you were allowed 12 ozs of sweets, this was if you could get them. Meat to the value of six pence in today's money, sausages were not rationed but were hard to get. Offal was not rationed in the beginning, but sometimes it was classed as part of the meat ration. A person I know had to beg her butcher to let her have a quarter of a pound of stewing meat, so that she could make dinners for her baby (no Heinz jars of ready meals then). Some of the grocers had their favourite customers and kept food for them 'under the counter'. People did not forget this after the war and they never again patronised the grocer. Tinned ham and salmon soon became unavailable, although Spam was to be had. Later on in the war soap and washing powder along with coal was also rationed. All sorts of things were burned on the fire and wet tea leaves were used to keep the fire going overnight. Fish was not rationed, but it was in short supply, because our fishing grounds were being patrolled by German U Boats.

The General Buff coloured Ration Book included pages of different coloured coupons one for each item of grocery. There was a different Ration Book for an expectant mother, a certificate had to be issued by a doctor, certified midwife or health visitor to obtain one of these. Extra meat and eggs were allowed. Welfare clinics distributed orange juice, cod liver oil capsules, vitamins and iron tablets. When the birth of the baby had been registered, a new Ration Book was issued.

On the radio (wireless as it was then called), The Radio Doctor, Charles Hill, would advise on Nutrition and Health and how to keep fit on your weekly rations. The writer has recently seen a photograph of him, he looked very well fed! Doctor Hill was the Secretary of the British Medical Association, the organisation that represented family doctors. When the National Health Service Bill was published, it was said that he had wanted to strangle the NHS from birth. He seems a nice kind of man.

People were encouraged to grow vegetables, as these were the mainstay of the daily diet. *Dig for Victory* leaflets were available to help with the gardening. There was a film entitled *A Garden goes to War*, and a children's booklet *Happy Hours on the Food Front*. The book described how daddy, in the Home Guard and not in the Forces, enjoyed working in the garden growing vegetables. To catch the children's attention there was Doctor Carrot and Potato Pete, this was to encourage them to eat their vegetables. Here is a little ditty about Potato Pete.

Potatoes new and Potatoes old
Potatoes in a salad, cold
Potatoes baked or mashed or fried
Potatoes whole, potato pied
Enjoy them all including chips
Remembering spuds don't come in ships

I can remember my mother and aunts bottling fruit and salting runner beans in jars.

How about the programmes on the wireless, such as:- *ITMA* (It's that man again), with Tommy Handley, *The Brains Trust*, this went on air for the first time on the 1st January 1941 and Music While you Work, was relayed by a loudspeaker across the factory floor. Then there was *Worker's Playtime*, this was first broadcast on the 31st May 1941 and it was on three times a week broadcast from various factory canteens. There was also *The Robinson's* and Wilfred Pickles along with Mabel in *Have a Go*. People would take gramophones into the air-raid shelters with them, no need for electricity, just wind up the handle! They would all have a singsong, this was considered good for morale. I will take you back to the past by naming some of the songs such as: *A Lovely Way to Spend an Evening, A Nightingale Sang in Berkeley Square, I've Heard That Song Before, I'll Get By (as long as I have you), Moonlight Becomes You, The Very Thought of You, There I've Said It Again, When the Lights Go on Again All Over the World, You always Hurt the One you Love* and one of my old favourites, *You'll Never Know Just How Much I Love You* (How romantic!). Of course there were many more. But I hope that this will help the readers to cast their minds back and think about their memories.

I am sure that you will remember some of the singers of the war such as:-Vera Lynn, Anne Shelton, Al Bowlly, The Andrew Sisters, Gracie Fields and Betty Driver, she sang with Henry Hall's Band (Yes, she is the one who is in Coronation Street). The entertainers were a big part of people's lives. It took their minds off rationing, blackout and the threat of invasion.

The younger generation frequented the dance halls. There were many dance bands at this time. Ivy Benson and her Orchestra, was formed in 1939 of all female musicians and was one of the top bands of this era. Other well known bands and orchestras were Geraldo and his Orchestra, Joe Loss, Harry Roy, Carroll Gibbons, Edmundo Ros and his Rumba Band and of course Victor Silvester (strictly tempo). Oh! They don't have music like this now. I bet a lot of you ladies 'Jitter-Bugged' (and probably still can!), at The GEC, The Matrix, Alfred Herbert's, Courtaulds, The Savoy, The

Rialto Casino, The Drill Hall, Neal's Ballroom and The Standard, Banner Lane Ballroom. There was also a ballroom upstairs in The Fire Station in the city. I hope this brings back some memories. I was told that about fifty per cent of the ladies met their husbands at the dance halls.

Going to the cinema was very popular and I am sure that many of you would have seen, *Gone with the Wind*, (1939) starring Vivien Leigh and Clarke Gable, *Wicked Lady* (1945) featuring Margaret Lockwood and James Mason, *In Which We Serve*, (1942) with that wonderful actor John Mills and Kaye Walsh, *Millions Like Us* (1943) with Eric Porter and Patricia Roc. One weepy that springs to mind is *Waterloo Bridge*, (1940) starring Vivien Leigh and Robert Taylor. We must not forget *Mrs. Miniver* with Greer Garson, (1942). This film was produced to raise the morale of the population. *Fanny By Gaslight*, (1944) featuring Phyllis Calvert and Stewart Granger, *The Seventh Veil* (1945) with Ann Todd, *The Man in Grey* (1943) with James Mason. One of my favourite films was *Now Voyager* (1942) with Bette Davis, Claude Rains, Gladys Cooper and Paul Henreid, particularly the scene towards the end with the cigarette. After the war in 1946 came *Brief Encounter* starring Trevor Howard and Celia Johnson, there was not a dry eye in the cinema. Of course there were many more films. No violence or pornography in those days!

There were many magazines published at this time. *Woman's Own, Woman, Woman's Weekly* and *Picture Post*. I bet the old magazines had a different content to what they have now. Some of the comics were *Film Fun, Beano, Tiny Tots, Radio Fun, The Wizard* and many more. Boy's had magazines such as *The Champion, Boy's Own, The Rover* and *Hotspur*. I can remember having the *Girls Crystal* and I could not wait for the next issue, so I could continue with the serial, as it was always left as a cliff-hanger. Also published at the time was *The Children's Newspaper*, which was interesting as it dealt with current affairs and was written in such a way that children could understand. Of course the papers and magazines had to be saved for the salvage collection to help towards the war effort. If you were found burning them you were fined.

Gas masks made a wonderful fashion accessory; everyone was issued with one. Children had 'Mickey Mouse' ones and babies had a gas helmet, which completely covered them. Filtered air was pumped into it by means of hand bellows. The babies looked like aliens from outer-space. A friend of mine loaned me a Gas Mask and on it is printed S.G and Co. Ltd., Aug. 1938. They look the most frightening appliances. I wonder how many times people had to use them? I am led to believe that they were only used for practice runs.

5

Many people had air raid shelters in their gardens. Anderson shelters were made of corrugated steel and normally half was below ground level. The half that protruded above the ground was covered with soil and soon became covered with weeds and grass. From the air the shelter was invisible. They always appeared to be cold and damp. Morrison shelters, for indoor use, were like large steel tables and went together like Meccano sets. The council would deliver them to your homes and it was up to the family to put it together.

Everyone had to carry an Identity Card. If it was lost, damaged or defaced it had to be reported at once to the National Registration Office. If an Identity Card was found it had to be handed into a police station or the National Registration Office. Failure to do this was an offence punishable by a fine or imprisonment or both.

In December 1941 conscription was introduced for unmarried women between the ages of 18 and 30. They could either go into industry, which usually meant munitions work, the women's services or the civil defence. Men did not like the idea of women working on the factory floor as they always thought of it as being a male occupation, but then they had no alternative, as this was war. Women worked on the Railways doing such jobs as porters, carriage cleaners and ticket collectors. They also worked as mechanics and platelayers. Women worked for the Post Office as cable repairers and motorcycle messengers. They also worked on the buses and trams and became conductors. This became the turning point for women, as they had now found freedom and still have it to this day.

Women joined many organisations to help with the war effort. The Women's Land Army, these women came from all walks of life. (See our publication 'Telling Tales' for articles about the Land Army). Lady Reading who was responsible for the Women's Land Army, was also the founder of The Women's Voluntary Service (WVS). Pearl Hyde who later became the first woman Lord Mayor of Coventry organised the WVS in Coventry. (See our publication 'Redressing the Balance'). A relative of mine joined the WVS in 1941, when she was working at The Standard Motor Company. She and her friend took on the duty of manning a disused sub-station at the top of Broomfield Road, Earlsdon, Coventry; this was fitted with a tap, a gas ring and a few chairs and tables. They served firemen that were on duty, with tea or cocoa; coffee was not available at this time. She will never forget making the cocoa in a big enamel bucket – this put her off cocoa for life!

Many children were evacuated; plans were made for them to be taken by their teachers into the countryside where they were billeted in private houses and shared local school accommodation. Besides school children, provision was made for blind and other disabled people and for mothers, who had children under school age, to be taken into the country. Most villages were only a short distance from Coventry, such as Kenilworth, Meriden, Corley and Fillongley. What wonderful people to open up their homes to complete strangers. I have spoken to people who were evacuated and they told me that for years after they still kept in contact with the people that they were evacuated with.

If your home was bombed, then you could claim War Damage Compensation, there was a guide published for the *Householder, Landlord, Shopkeeper* and *Businessman*. I think that you would have needed a degree to understand the implications of what you could or could not claim for. People who had lost their homes were probably in a state of shock, without having to read the technical legal terms.

The products you do not see these days, although we have memories of them are:-

Kellogg's Wheat Flakes, Welgar Shredded Wheat, Cremo Oats, Mazawattee Tea, Fry's Breakfast Cocoa, Coleman's Vitacup (Tonic Food Beverage), Drew's Self-raising flour. What about household cleaning materials such as, Rinso, Oxydol, Crysella Soap Flakes, Sylvan Flakes, Vim, Jiffy Dyes and Shinio Metal Polish.

The writer hopes that this article will stir up some memories and get you talking.

'BE LIKE DAD, KEEP MUM'   'CARELESS TALK COSTS LIVES'

Angela Atkin

Bibliography
We Remember – Coventry Archives Educational Service
The Wartime Scrapbook – Robert Opie
Book called *We'll meet again* – Vera Lynn
Readers Digest – *Yesterday's Britain*

A Coventry Schoolgirl at War

In May 1939 I had my eleventh birthday. I only had three months left at Stoke Heath School before we all had to move on, as there were only infant and junior sections. I had passed the scholarship examination and was to start at Stoke Park School in September. Stoke Park and Barrs Hill were then Council owned girls' grammar schools, to complement King Henry VIII and Bablake boys' schools. The school uniform was very strict; Mum and I visited Bendall's in White Street (roughly where the Ring Road flyover is now) to obtain blouses, tie, gymslip, hat, black overall for science, white overall for domestic science, navy blue coat, etc. So I was kitted out.

Dad had decided that his business was now sufficiently prosperous to allow us a fortnight's holiday, instead of the one week we had previously enjoyed. We now also possessed a Morris 8 car, superior and faster than the previous Jowett. So accommodation was booked in Newquay, Cornwall and we set off in mid-August 1939. By this time war was becoming ever more threatening and Mum and Dad kept a careful check on the news. On Thursday of the second week, they decided that we should return home. On arrival, we found that the bus windows were all covered in blue paint to stop light escaping. Neighbours were advising each other where black curtain material could be obtained, as all were convinced that the war was about to start, which of course it did on 3rd September, the day on which we should have returned from holiday.

Most schools had evacuation plans. Stoke Heath was going to Edgehill, Stoke Park to Leamington. Stoke Park would only take existing pupils, not those who were about to start, so I could only go with Stoke Heath (who as mentioned had no seniors). Dad said that this was no good, as I would not learn anything, so I stayed at home. Quite soon, Stoke Park reopened for a few hours each week to cater for the new intake and the older girls who had not joined the evacuation. We went in for a couple of hours each time and were given homework to complete and take in on our next visit. Stoke Park School was then in Brays Lane where Sacred Heart School is now. The girls who had gone to Leamington quickly began to return as there were no air raids at this time. By the start of the second term (beginning of 1940) school was open full time and things were fairly normal, apart from the news being totally dominated by the war and men being called up for military service. My only cousin was eighteen years old in 1939; he was apprenticed to an electrical engineering company in Birmingham, where the manager of the apprentices was an officer in the Territorial Army and therefore persuaded the lads to join up. My cousin was called up within the first fortnight of the outbreak of war. He was initially in the Royal Artillery and was stationed at various anti-aircraft sites, including Tile Hill and Binley, in Coventry. After a while a new regiment was formed - the REME (Royal Electrical & Mechanical Engineers) to which he was transferred. Then it transpired that someone was needed to train new recruits in New Zealand, he was chosen and shipped off there for the remainder of the war.

Food and clothing rationing started, but I can't give dates for these. A small amount of meat was padded out with more vegetables (doubtless good for us). Fish, I think, was not rationed, but Mum had to queue to get some. We were issued with gas masks which we had to carry about, but fortunately never had to use.

The government were providing households with Anderson shelters made from sections of corrugated iron, to protect people during air raids. It was necessary to dig a large hole, about three feet deep, erect the shelter in it, then pile all the earth back on top. However, we were not entitled to one of these handouts (something to do with Dad having his own business) and they were not available for sale. Dad consulted our jobbing builder who showed him some plans for a brick-built shelter and he agreed to have one. So in early autumn 1940, about half of the lawn was dug up and the brick walls were built, starting about 3ft or so down in the ground. A concrete floor and roof were added, but the shelter started to fill with water. The builders had hit a thin layer of sand with a trickle of water flowing through. The problem was never overcome, so on the night of the blitz, 14th November 1940, we were in the street shelter. These were windowless brick structures built straight onto the road, without lighting or heating, so much safer than a house.

We lived at the corner of Shakespeare Street and Avon Street and there was a lot of damage in our area, including five or six deaths and various injuries. We were fortunate to remain uninjured, but our house was badly damaged, without a roof or windows. The road was covered with earth, glass, roof slates and tiles, bricks, etc. Some houses had been completely demolished. We walked down Shakespeare Street, as we had friends near the Walsgrave Road end. The lower end of the road had no damage whatsoever, not so much as a broken pane of glass. Our friends made us very welcome.

We decided that we should try to leave Coventry, as it was feared that the German bombers might return quickly and take advantage of ruptured water mains and disruption caused by the blitz, but how to leave was the problem. The car could not be used, as only priority occupations were allowed petrol. Many roads were impassable and the town centre was covered in rubble, so I don't think there were any buses. Dad decided to go and check on his shop, which was fortunately untouched. Somehow, he managed to discover

9

that there were some trains at Berkswell station. A friend of his, who had a plumbing supplies business, said that his lorry driver would run us there. So we set off, Mum and I in the cab with the driver, Dad and my brother on the back with a bath for company! We had decided to try to get to Wolverhampton, where Mum's uncle and aunt lived. After a while, a Birmingham-bound train arrived. On arrival at New Street Station the tannoy announced that an air raid was in progress, so we had to go down into the subway. Eventually, a train for Wolverhampton was announced and we continued our journey. All was quiet on arrival and we caught a bus to the home of Mum's uncle and aunt, arriving at about 10.30pm. The journey had taken about eight hours. They were not one bit surprised to see us and welcomed us in.

Kathleen Barker

After a couple of days Dad decided he must return to Coventry to reopen his shop. He slept at the friends' house in Shakespeare Street; only the husband remained there, as his wife and young son had gone to an aunt's house in Bradford. Mum, my brother and I stayed in Wolverhampton for about two to three weeks, then Dad found that the family who lived at 4 Burlington Road in Coventry had found some sort of accommodation in the countryside and were happy to let their house. So we all returned to Coventry, where we joined Dad at the friends' house for a few nights, whilst we sorted through the mess of our home. We found that most of the furniture could be used once it had been cleaned. Much of the crockery was smashed to bits, including the best full tea service (twelve of everything). This had been kept in a glass-fronted cabinet, which was totally destroyed. Another casualty was a delicately carved ivory Chinese houseboat, which stood on an oval ebony base and was covered with a glass dome. Only a little earlier, an insurance man who had called, offered Mum fifty pounds on the spot for this, but of course she said she could not possibly sell it. Surveying the wreckage, the base covered with white powder and bits of glass, Mum said, 'I wish I had taken my fifty pounds!'

Transport was the next requirement. All that could be obtained was a horse and cart owned by Mr Clews. He made a number of trips and all the serviceable items were removed to Burlington Road. This house was smaller than ours and did not have a bathroom, but with so many houses destroyed or uninhabitable, no one could pick and choose; at least we had a home again and it was very near to Dad's shop.

As we started to move around again, we discovered which areas had been badly hit and which had little or no damage. The town centre had suffered badly and the cathedral had been burnt out. Stoke Park School was 21years old in 1940, and early in November all staff and pupils walked to the cathedral for a commemorative service. This must have been amongst the last few services to be held there.

Following our return Mum called at the school to explain my absence. She was informed that a new evacuation had been arranged to Atherstone and it was suggested that I should go; Mum agreed. However, when she told me, I protested and said that I was not going. I said, 'Look mum, we nearly all got killed; if we are going to get killed, let's get killed together.' The prospect of life as an orphan certainly did not appeal! Mum protested that she had agreed that I should go, but I said again, 'I am not going. I don't care what you have told the teacher, I am not going.' So I returned to Brays Lane at the beginning of term in January 1941 and the gym mistress said, 'What are you doing here? Miss Smith and I walked round Atherstone in the pouring rain, finding lodgings for you.' I explained that we very nearly got killed and that if we were going to be killed, I wanted us to be together. Anyway, things gradually settled down and I found that a lot of the girls were still in Coventry. I think about a quarter of the pupils had gone to Atherstone.

We had numerous air raids, but the only other really severe one was in April 1941. This was not as bad as the November blitz, but certainly bad enough. The house in Burlington Road was equipped with an Anderson shelter, so we felt much safer. The only damage we suffered was a few broken windows, which were soon replaced.

At school, we had underground trenches, which had been dug into the lawn. Occasionally the sirens would sound and we would march down there. Lessons were supposed to continue, but it was not possible to do much without desks and blackboards, and all pupils sitting in a long line on benches. However, this did not take up much school time as nothing serious happened in the daytime, for all significant air raids were at night.

The school uniform could not be kept up to its previous high standard, as we did not have sufficient clothing coupons, also various items became less and less available. As we got older we were loath to use the precious coupons on school uniform, so we would do our utmost to make it last out. During domestic science lessons, we had been taught how to do the correct type of patches for various purposes. This was extremely useful for the elbows of blouses, as one blouse could be sacrificed to provide the material for patching the others. The other option was to turn long sleeves into short sleeves. One spot of very good fortune occurred when an older girl who lived down the road left school and her mother asked mine if she was interested in buying Joan's uniform for me. Mum snapped it up and it just about lasted out until I left.

We were encouraged to knit items for the forces, such as mittens, socks and scarves. The mittens were knitted on four needles, a bit tricky but at least there was no sewing up to do at the end; the tricky bit on the socks was turning the heel! Make do and mend was another feature of life. Hand knitted jumpers that had been worn out at the elbows would be unpicked, the wool washed and then re-knitted into gloves or scarves, or two jumpers might become one striped jumper. Any leftover wool was knitted into squares for blankets.

Occasionally, something extra in the way of food would turn up. Two items I particularly remember were a rabbit and a Christmas chicken. They both came fully clothed! We found some instructions in Mrs Beeton's book and on both occasions Mum said, 'You have a go!' I managed it and both items tasted very good; I have never skinned a rabbit or plucked a chicken since then.

Whilst at Burlington Road, a local cat decided that she would like to live with us. We discovered who the cat belonged to, and as she would not settle with this family, it was agreed that we should have her. At this time a portion of the meat ration had to be taken as corned beef, which was supplied to the butchers in very long tins. The premises on the corner of Swan Lane and Burlington Road was a butcher's shop and his garden ran alongside Burlington Road, ending at the side of our house. Mr Stanbridge, the butcher, dumped the empty tins at the bottom of his garden.

On a lovely summer morning, the doors had been left open. Mum and I were in the house and we heard a noise in the kitchen. I peered in to find the cat had a large rodent in her mouth. I presumed that it was a rat, although I had never seen one. Knowing Mum would be alarmed, I asked how big a mouse was. Mum indicated with her fingers - something about six inches including the tail. 'Oh!' I said, 'Then the cat's caught a rat.' Mother panicked. 'Shut the door, don't let the cat in here.' Calming down a little, she then said, 'Go and ask Mr Stanbridge to come and help the cat kill the rat, it's come out of his corned beef tins.' I asked how she knew this, but she just replied, 'Of course that's where it's come from.' Protesting would be of no avail, so off I went. The shop was busy, so I stood by the till.

Mr Stanbridge asked what I wanted. I said 'Our cat has caught a large rat and Mum says that it has come out of your corned beef tins, so please will you come and help the cat to kill it.' 'And how does your mother know the rat has come out of my corned beef tins?' he enquired. 'I don't know,' I replied, 'but that's what she said.' He agreed to come and we went in through the garden gate. Startled by our entrance, the cat let go of the rat. It ran round and round the butcher's feet, followed by the cat, then rat and cat ran down the garden path and down into the Anderson shelter. The butcher asked for a garden spade, which I supplied, then waited at the entrance to the shelter until the rat appeared again, when he gave it a good whack. The cat picked up her trophy and finished it off. Mum then appeared at the kitchen door, all smiles, to thank Mr Stanbridge for his help.

We lived in Burlington Road for nearly three years, by which time our Shakespeare Street house had been repaired and it was time to return. My brother had become Dad's assistant at the shop, so they were both occupied there, leaving Mum and I to deal with the move. We had a proper removal van this time. Mum went in the van and I was instructed to take the cat in her basket, keeping her covered so that she could not see where she was going. I obeyed instructions, but need not have bothered as that cat had no intention of leaving us. She was so troubled that we might move again that she only went out into the garden when she absolutely had to, then shot back indoors at top speed: of course she gradually settled down again. Most of the neighbours returned, those whose houses were less severely damaged had already returned before us. Where complete rebuilds were required, the people had a much longer wait.

In November 1943 my brother had his 18th birthday, which meant that he would be 'called up.' He had taken the precaution of joining the Air Training Corps, which would enable him to get into the ground staff of the Royal Air Force. About a month after his birthday his call-up papers arrived and off he went. After training to service aircraft, he was stationed at airfields in Kent, Yorkshire and Northumberland, then later in Germany and Burma. He was demobbed a little over two years later.

We had no holidays during the war; in fact travelling anywhere was quite difficult. To visit my uncle and aunt in Birmingham, we had to join the queue for the Midland Red bus at the old Pool Meadow bus station. Trains were notoriously late. When my brother managed to get home for a couple of days, we would go to the station to see him off; it was not unusual for the train to be two hours late.

For entertainment, most people went to the cinema at least once a week. It was cheap and there were so many cinemas in Coventry (and everywhere else) that you could always find a film that you wished to see; also the programme included a newsreel from which we could see what was happening on the war fronts. We could go for a walk even after dark, without fear of being molested. Cycling was enjoyable as there was little traffic on the roads; only one slight problem was that all the signposts had been removed, that was because signposts would have helped the enemy if there had been an invasion. So sometimes we took a wrong turning and added a few miles to our route.

I left school in July 1944 and commenced work at the Inland Revenue office. This was just after D-Day and the war was entering its final stages, with Germany surrendering in May 1945, followed by Japan in August 1945. My cousin was able to leave the army almost immediately; he had married before going to New Zealand and had a son. He commenced work with the Royal Radar Establishment (RRE), so continuing his army work into civilian life. The cat remained with us to her dying day. Dad reached a compromise with the builder and the water-filled air raid shelter was demolished and buried, the earth replaced on top of it and the lawn relayed.

So was it a good time to be a schoolgirl? In some ways obviously 'No.' Air raids were most unpleasant and dangerous and friends and acquaintances were killed and injured, also everyone had relatives and friends in the armed forces and were worried for their safety. However, in other ways 'Yes.' We quickly got our priorities right, it was people who were important, not possessions. Money did not play so large a part as it does now. The shops were not filled with the latest fashions as now and in any case, clothes could only be obtained to the extent for which we had coupons. We were much more equal.

Even now, after all these years, we are troubled by the way younger people discard clothes and other goods simply because they are no longer in fashion. As one friend remarked to me recently, 'The trouble with us is, we were brought up when there was a war on.'

Kathleen Barker

Emma Blunn

Emma Blunn, known as Emmie, was born in Radcliffe, near Manchester, on 5 December 1918. She was the eldest of three, her two brothers, Albert and Wilfred being a few years younger. Her father was a soldier in the 1914-18 war when he married her mother. When the war was over employment was very hard to find and he had various jobs, making black puddings for a local butcher and selling ice-cream to name but a few. They all lived with Emmie's grandmother, who was a very strict Victorian and ruled the household with a rod of iron. She had little time for her son-in-law and caused so much friction he left his wife and children and found a job in Manchester. Emmie's mother was frightened of her own mother and refused to leave and go with her husband. Emmie went to the Methodist School in Radcliffe when she was three years old, sometimes in the morning, sometimes in the afternoon. These were the days before free school milk but Emmie's teacher, Miss Gillan, used to heat up milk on a gas ring and give it to the children. The school also had small camp beds where the little ones could have a sleep. Emmie's father kept in touch with the family and saw them at Christmas and birthdays bringing them presents but her grandmother would not let him in! When Emmie's grandmother died, her father, who was by this time working for the General Electric Company (GEC) in Manchester, was transferred to Coventry so Emmie's mother and father got back together and came to live in Coventry.

Emmie's first job at the age of fourteen years old was making buttered brazils in a sweet factory. When they moved to Coventry in 1935 she was sixteen years old and Emmie started work at the GEC factory in Uxbridge Avenue in the Stoke District of Coventry, but was transferred to GEC Ford Street and then Queen Victoria Road and worked there until the Blitz in 1940. She worked on the track in the factory fitting dials to the black telephones, moving on to grinding the small pieces of metal for the earpiece of the handsets, these had to be an exact level and measured on a gauge to check the depth. When she moved to Queen Victoria Road she worked on the wiring of the telephones for the General Post Office (GPO).

Mrs May Hallworth, Emmie's mother, had a good eye for property to rent and in the five years until the Blitz they moved five times. Their first house was in Grafton Street, then Mrs Hallworth spotted a nice house in Sewall Highway, so they moved there. The next move was to 22 Longfellow Road. Mrs Hallworth was a spiritualist and she became friendly with a lady who lived in Holyhead Road, so she spied a house to rent in Eastlands Grove and they packed their belongings and moved there. However, there was problems with damp so they moved to Norman Place Road in Coundon and were living there when the war started. They had a half-size billiard table and Emmie and her two brothers used to play billiards. When the air raids were on they used to shelter under the billiard table. It was not long before Mrs Hallworth had itchy feet again and wished she was back in Stoke. She saw an advertisement in the Telegraph for a house in Tennyson Road (this was backing on to their old house in Longfellow Road). The key had to be collected from a local newsagent. So, that evening, Emmie and her mother collected the key and looked round the house by torchlight. Her mother liked what she saw so off they were again, moving house and Emmie stayed there until she was married.

Emmie hated having to go into work to inform them of her change of address. She suspected the Company thought her family had not paid the rent so they had to move! Of course this was not the case.

Emmie joined the Air Raid Precautions (ARP) while working at the GEC. She worked on the top floor of the building in Queen Victoria Road works which was a large building three storeys high. She studied for her First Aid Certificate for St Johns Ambulance. As part of their duties they had to practice evacuating the building in an air raid and coping with anyone who had been injured. As Emmie was the smallest in the class of twelve she had to be the `injured person' secured to the stretcher. As the fire escape was an iron staircase on the outside of the building Emmie was very scared! She was carried down three flights at precarious angles wondering what would happen if they dropped her over the edge! The evacuation point was at the back of the building where Fyffes stored the green bananas ready to sell in the market when they were ripe. When she was doing ARP duties she insisted on wearing trousers as it was much more convenient when running up and down stairs. Her mother had definite Victorian ideas about young ladies wearing trousers so to get round this dilemma Emmie smuggled her trousers into work and changed there to do her ARP duty and then changed back to come home.

Another time they were taken into a room in the yard where a small green pellet was broken. This was mustard gas and everyone had to get used to wearing their gas mask and to experience what it would be like should there be an attack using mustard gas. Gas masks were issued to everyone, children as well as adults. This training was invaluable when she eventually had a daughter as she had practiced using the gas cots for babies. This was a small cot and the baby was placed inside and covered for protection against gas. Then fresh air had to be pumped into the cot so that the baby could breathe and be kept alive. Fortunately Emmie did not have to use the gas mask as they were quite unpleasant to wear as the rubber stuck to your face and the visor steamed up after a while and you could not see where you were going.

In the early years of the war Emmie often went to the pictures with a girlfriend in the blackout. There was no street lighting and the few cars on the road only had narrow slits for headlights. Armed with just a torch, she thought nothing of walking into town in the pitch black darkness carrying her handbag and her gas mask in its special stylish bag, her mother had bought her, which was white with black edging. Often when she was watching the picture it would come up on the screen that a raid was imminent and the sirens had gone but if you wished to stay in your seat the picture would continue. She always stayed and hoped for the best but never felt frightened!

Emma and Jimmy Blunn

Emmie married Jimmy Blunn on 19 October 1940, just before the Coventry Blitz on 14 November. They were married at the local church, Stoke St Michaels, which was not far from her home in Tennyson Road at three o'clock in the afternoon. The wedding car took the bride, groom and family to Buckleys, the photographers on Gosford Green. These were black and white photographs which were professionally tinted. However, items were often changed by mistake. Jimmy's mother had given Emmie a necklace with a horse-shoe which had a sprig of white heather through it. When the photographs were ready to be collected, the necklace had turned into a cross and chain and her beautiful bouquet of red roses had been transformed into pink carnations!

The wedding reception was held at St Margaret's Hall on Ball Hill. Emmie had two bridesmaids - her friend, Jenny Patterson who she worked with at the GEC and Jimmy's sister. The best man was Emmie's brother, Albert. Emmie's friend, Lil Ashton, took a group photograph and also one of the wedding cake. This was a fruit cake covered in dark chocolate and decorated with white doves and cupids. As they were married at the start of the war things were not as restrictive as they were later on.

As it got dark the sirens went but the party was still in full swing so everyone carried on enjoying themselves. However, the wardens came and insisted everyone had to go home as bombs were dropping. All the guests went to their homes and Jimmy and Emmie prepared to walk to Leicester Causeway to their new home which would take them about an hour to reach. This house belonged to a friend of her mother who had moved out of Coventry and had agreed to rent the property to Emmie and her new husband.

They started to walk to their new home, Emmie was still in her wedding dress and silver shoes. As they were walking, a plane came over and they had to dive into a brick shelter in Clay Lane. Unfortunately the shelter was half full of water so poor Emmie's dress and shoes were soaked. However, the plane passed over so they continued to walk to Leicester Causeway. Emmie's friend from work, Lil Ashton, also lived in Leicester Causeway but she left Coventry each night to go to Rugby or Brinklow to escape the bombing. This was a common occurrence in Coventry during the war and crowds of people would trudge along the Binley Road to get out of the city. A few cars were on the road so a few were fortunate to get a lift. Lil had told Emmie that there was a shelter in their back garden so if there was a raid they could use that. Tired and exhausted they eventually reached their house but as the raid was still going on they had to spend their wedding night in the Anderson shelter with the neighbours, Emmie still in her wedding finery! It finally became light and the All Clear sounded so Jimmy and Emmie made their way to their house only to find their friends had put confetti all over the windows and there was a huge chamber pot on view with JUST MARRIED on it. The next day Jimmy went back to work at the Daimler factory; in those days there was not time for a honeymoon.

Leicester Causeway was only a short-term home as it was furnished and after a week, Emmie's mother-in-law told her of an empty house in Stubbs Grove, just around the corner from their house in Alfall Road. It was the first house in the cul-de-sac. They moved on Saturday, 9 November 1940, and settled in. They did not furnish upstairs but concentrated on making the bedroom in one of the downstairs rooms as a safeguard against air raids. On Thursday night, 14 November, Jimmie was on Home Guard duty. As Jimmy's family only lived around the corner his youngest brother always came round to keep Emmie company while Jimmy was doing guard duty and to have his dinner. Emmie had been busy preparing the meal and doing the washing in the big gas boiler. Jimmy came home and almost immediately the siren went to warn of an imminent air raid. They crowded in the alcove under the stairs to shelter. It was very frightening as the noise of the aeroplanes and the bombs dropping was horrendous. They could also see the flares coming down. However, it seemed that they had escaped as it suddenly went very quiet, then everything shuddered, clouds of dust and smoke were everywhere, a landmine had dropped into Emmie's back garden! The whole of the back of the house came tumbling down. Fortunately the only injury was a cut ear for Jimmy. They scrambled out of the house and ran up the road; it was like daylight with all the fires and explosions.

Jimmy's brother had received such a fright he had already rushed home to his mother but they met him coming back to see if they were alright. They spent the rest of the night in a brick shelter. The next day they went back to their house to see just what damage had been caused. The back of the house was completely gone but the front of the house was still standing. Most things were smashed, the wedding cake, in boxes ready to be sent to relatives and friends was ruined, although the copper was still full of washing! The stairs had gone and showing on the pantry shelves was a plate with a perfect round hole through it. There was also a tin of salmon, which Emmie had been saving for a special occasion, with a hole through that. They managed to save the bed and the chest of drawers but everything else was smashed. Several months afterwards Emmie went back to look at her old house and everything was the same but this time she rescued the washing, rewashed it and was able to wear it for some time to come. Her two brothers managed to rescue the bed and chest of drawers on an old handcart and these formed the basis of her new home. In those days nothing was wasted!

So after just three weeks of married life Emmie was made homeless. They went to her mother's house in Tennyson Road but as the raids were very frequent Emmie and her mother went to Manchester to stay with her Aunty Kate until other accommodation could be arranged for them. After a few weeks Jimmy telephoned to say he had found a house in Hinckley for them to live in. Emmie was due to start work at the Dunlop as everyone had to work in those days when she found she was expecting her first baby. Jean was born in February 1942 and they stayed in Hinckley until Jean was nine months old. Emmie was desperate to get back to Coventry to her friends and family and was delighted when Jimmy's mother let them know that a house was becoming vacant in Siddeley Avenue. She, Jimmy and baby Jean moved into their new home in October 1942 and it has been their home to this day for sixty-five years.

They applied to the Council for help to furnish their new home. Jimmy's parents had bought them the dining room suite and her mother and father had bought the bedroom suite and all this furniture had been destroyed by the bomb. After much deliberation the man at the counter at Sibree Hall offered her £6. She was not amused and said there was no way she could furnish a house on £6. He tried to point out that he had to take into account wear and tear! Emmie replied that the furniture had had no wear and tear as they had only moved into the house on the Saturday, and on the Thursday night it was the Blitz and they had lost everything. After considering this Emmie was given £30 to set up her new home. Emmie managed to get a few bits of furniture and a square of lino from the second-hand department at Owen Owen's. They could not afford carpets in those days. Everything had to be scrubbed. Monday was washing day, Tuesday for ironing and mending anything and darning socks. Wednesday she scrubbed all the front flagstones from the front door to the pavement and all the flagstones at the back of the house, all through the hall.

Jimmy still worked at the Daimler but in Uttoxeter so he had to travel there and back every weekend. They always slept downstairs and when the sirens went she would gather Jean in her arms, wrap her in a blanket and run up the street to the brick shelter in Siddeley Avenue. Although these shelters were no protection against bombs dropping close by, they were safer than your home which could collapse on top of you.

In November 1944 Emmie's second daughter Mary was born. Eighteen months later, in May 1946, a third daughter, Catherine, was born to Emmie and Jimmy but sadly died in August, just over 2 months old, suffering from lobar pneumonia. Catherine had not been well and Emmie had taken her to the doctor who diagnosed a stomach upset and gave her some tablets. However, Catherine deteriorated rapidly and Emmie kept calling the doctor, only to be told he would come after surgery but he did not come. At that time there were no telephones in houses so someone had to keep walking to the nearest telephone box. Finally Emmie was told over the telephone to wrap her in a blanket and take her to hospital. They had to take her on the bus as the hospital was quite a way away. When they arrived at the hospital, the doctor was shocked at how frail Catherine was and told Emmie and Jimmy that she was too ill to be examined. They stayed with her at the hospital, but were told to go home and rest. However, soon afterwards a hospital worker came to tell them that Catherine was worse so they went back to the hospital. This happened, off and on, for a week. Finally they were summoned once more but this time Emmie could feel how cold Catherine was and she asked for more blankets. Emmie and Jimmy were asked to leave the room as the doctor had to examine the baby. Some time later they were told that Catherine had died. The doctor said that Catherine should have been admitted to hospital much sooner and Emmie pointed out that she and her husband had done everything they could to get the doctor to come to the house and see her. The hospital doctor asked if he could perform a post mortem on the baby to find out the cause of death and it was discovered that she had died of lobar pneumonia.

Emmie's youngest brother, Wilfred, was in the RAF and was killed in the war and is buried out in Africa. He had been in the Home Guard before joining up. Strange as it may seem, several years after the war had ended a man came to Emmie's door. He asked if Wilfred had been in the Home Guard and when Emmie answered in the affirmative he said he had come to collect his tin hat!

Times were hard for Emmie and Jimmy and their children during the war years. Food was rationed and a little bit of butter had to go a long way. If you were lucky to be at the shops when the tinned fruit was delivered to the local shop there was a huge queue and after a long wait they were rationed to the waiting customers. Similarly at the bakers; there were only certain days when cakes were available and queues were all down the street then you were only allowed one! When Emmie lived in Hinckley she often went to Leicester Market and sometimes it was possible to queue for a rabbit, so it was a great treat to have rabbit stew. Emmie's other favourites were fried spam and corned beef mash.

To make ends meet Emmie took a job as a cleaner in a large detached house for the owners of a local general store which sold most things including nightdresses and fruit and vegetables. She went every day to clean the house and received one pound per week. Through her contact with the family she started working in the shop itself although this was only now and again. So when another local shopowner, Ethel Bragg, asked Emmie to work full time in the nearby VG grocery store, she accepted. When Mrs Bragg sold the grocery shop, Emmie started to work in the shop next door, Whartons Newsagents, and continued working for Iris Harris, the manageress, until Iris retired.

Emmie had always been involved with the local community centre attending sewing classes and eventually sitting on the committee. They needed a cleaner at the Centre and someone to help George, the caretaker, who was diabetic, so Emmie applied for the job. They worked together for some time until George suffered a diabetic attack and was taken to hospital in a coma. As he was unfit to carry on his job, Emmie was made caretaker of the Community Centre. She went from cleaner to caretaker to theatre dresser to Wardrobe Mistress for Danny La Rue, the well-known entertainer. But that's another story!

Ann Waugh

Acknowledgements: Thank you to Emmie Blunn

Marjorie Campain (nee Campain)

Marjorie was in her last year at Barrs Hill Girls' Grammar School when war began. On leaving school, in 1940, she went to work at The Standard Motor Company on Fletchampstead Highway, in the offices, doing clerical work. After just one week, Marjorie's parents decided that she and her mother would go and stay in Lincolnshire with her grandparents as it was no longer safe to remain in Coventry. Her younger sister, Sylvia, was already there, attending school in Sleaford. At sixteen years of age you did not argue with your parents' decisions. So, as her father was to stay in Coventry, it was her older brother, Gordon, who drove them both to Lincolnshire. After just one week, it was obvious that the situation in Coventry was not going to alter, so back home came Marjorie with her mother. The following Monday Marjorie returned to her job at the Standard. On entering the office she was told that the boss wanted to see her. The boss asked his secretary to bring her shorthand book into his office and then proceeded to dictate, 'Miss Campain willfully left her work----- .' Wilfully left her work!! Marjorie was absolutely hopping mad, but again, a sixteen year old did not argue with the boss of a department. So, feeling her treatment to be very unjust, Marjorie went to the Employment Office and collected her cards. However, a neighbour, who worked at the Standard in Banner Lane as a Buyer's Secretary, was able to get her a job in the Ratefixing Department as a typist.

Her place of work was the big long Drawing Office. The length of the room was filled with drawing boards. The ratefixers were at the bottom end of this office facing the draughtsmen. Marjorie recalls that the man who sat opposite to her was a bit of a wag.

As Banner Lane was on the outskirts of Coventry, Marjorie, along with many other workers, travelled to and from work on the bus. She caught the bus at Hearsall Common and between here and the outskirts of the city at Banner Lane there were many factories, all producing equipment for the war effort. Marjorie remembers seeing many oil drums on the Common. Each of these drums contained a substance which, when lit by the soldiers, produced a large cloud of smoke. The objective of this smoke screen was to try to hide the factories from enemy aircraft flying overhead.

When the sirens went off to warn of a raid, Marjorie and her mother would go and sit under the stairs. Even there the noise of the aircraft going over was very loud. On one occasion she recalls her mother being most concerned about her father. Incendiaries were dropping everywhere, so most of the men were out fire watching, each ready with a bucket of sand to throw over the bombs when they landed. Her mother's concern continued to increase until poor Marjorie had to, tentatively, put her head round the door to see where her father was. Thankfully, all were safe.

As a teenager, Marjorie was very involved with the Church. There was always something going on; social occasions; discussion groups; dances. She was one of a group of youngsters who went to the Church so there was always company when walking back home. The Standard Cinema was another favourite haunt. Although her father had a car they were not able to use it very much because petrol was in such short supply. So visits to the family in Lincolnshire were few.

Marjorie came home for her dinner each day and then went back to work. On this day, when she came home, she found her mother crying. Thinking there had been some minor mishap, she asked, 'What's the matter?' Her mother replied, 'I think it's your brother.'

Her brother, Gordon, had joined the Royal Air Force in 1942, aged twenty years. He wanted to fly. Lucky enough to get his wish, he did part of his training at Cranwell and successfully achieved his wings. But, on January 13th,1943, on a small internal flight, his plane crashed and Gordon was killed. The effect this had on the family is still evident today. Some of Marjorie's most treasured possessions are mementos of her brother. A picture of him taken in his uniform, with his wings. A letter he sent to her on her eighteenth birthday – regretting that he could not be with her but promising her that he would take her to the Hippodrome, if she was a good girl, when he came home.

So many jobs in Coventry at the time were 'reserved occupations.' Consequently, it was mostly the young ones who went away - some never to return.

June Hill

My thanks go to Marjorie for taking the time and the trouble to talk to me about what was a very formative time of her life.
August 2007.

Doreen Howarth (nee Tudor)

Doreen was born in City Hospital, Birmingham and was one of five children, all girls. Her parents were Elsie and George Raynor Tudor her sisters were Florence, Mary, Dorothy and Georgina. Doreen, Florence and Mary attended St. Thomas' Church and school.

Doreen, Florence and Mary were evacuated the day before the war started, she cannot remember to where, just a farm in the country, but they were with two very strict and uncaring women. We must remember that the children were very young. They had to work picking apples and fruit and then had to carry them in large white enamel buckets, which were filled to the brim, back to the house. They did not stay there long before they went back home and then the bombing started.

The family were bombed out of their homes three times. They sheltered under the kitchen table and at one time were buried alive and had to be dug out by the Air Raid Precaution (ARP) wardens. She vividly remembers the heaps of rubble, where buildings had been destroyed by the enemy, and seeing bed linen and clothes hanging from the branches of trees. After the third time of being bombed out they were taken to a police station and spent the night on rough coconut mats. The family then moved to 30 William Street, which was just off Broad Street, Birmingham.

Doreen, Florence and Mary were evacuated again. She can remember her mother taking her to the railway station, Doreen wearing a label with her name, address and date of birth pinned on to her coat. She carried a few belongings in a brown paper bag, and, of course, her gas mask. She can remember hanging out of the carriage window, as the train was pulling away from the platform, and her mother telling her that she would come and fetch her. This must have been very traumatic for the children, particularly as they were so young. The children eventually arrived at Moira, Leicestershire, and were taken to St. Hilda's Church Hall and given food and drinks. They were then lined up, boys in one queue and the girls in another. Women started to come into the hall to choose which children would be suitable for them. A lady called Mrs. Wright, and her daughter, picked out Doreen and another girl called Grace and took them home to their cottage. Doreen was put into the bath in front of the fire and scrubbed and then both put into bed. A little time later she was brought downstairs and there were two other ladies and Mrs. Wright said 'You can have this little one; she won't be any good to me'. Doreen was then dressed and went, holding hands with them; she was very frightened as it was dark walking down the lane with the trees looking foreboding. Eventually, they arrived at a cottage where there were two men, one in a sailor's uniform who happened to be the fiancé of one of the ladies who was called Rose. The other lady, asked to be called Aunt Til, and her husband was to be called Uncle Jim. Once again she was put into the bath and given another good scrub. That night she slept in a big bed between Aunt Til and Rose.

Doreen and Aunt Til

Doreen had no idea where Florrie and Mary were taken to, but she later heard that they were living in separate places. She did see her sisters, but only occasionally.

The next day Aunt Til took her to the village shop and the assistant, who was called Betty asked 'How are you getting on with Aunt Til and Uncle Jim?' The headmaster took Doreen to Moira Council School. She really liked living in the countryside, wandering in the fields and making friends with the village children. Doreen said that she had an idyllic childhood, but at night felt traumatised and wanted her mummy. When Uncle Jim came home from work with a very black face she thought he was a sweep, but learned that he was a miner. Two of Doreen's uncles (who were her father's brothers), came from Birmingham to take Florrie and Mary back. When they called at Aunt Til's cottage she said 'Leave Doreen with us'. It was to be many years before she heard from Florrie and Mary again.

Doreen wrote to her mother every week and often asked Aunt Til 'When is Mummy coming?' Aunt Til always told her it was difficult for her to visit because of the war

Doreen thinks she was about nine years of age when she was given a box of chocolates by her teacher. She thought that it was a prize as she was the only one to receive them. When she finished school and was going home, being proud of having the chocolates, a girl called Phyllis told her that the only reason she was given them was because her mummy was dead. Doreen pushed the chocolates into the girl's hands and said 'You have them', and ran home. Aunt Til saw that she was distressed and asked her what the matter was; she sat her on her knee and told her that her mummy had gone to Jesus. Her mother, father and two small sisters had been killed during an air raid while in a shelter in Holliday Street, Birmingham. This was on the 11th December 1940.

When she was about 12 years of age and still living at the cottage with Aunt Til and Uncle Jim a children's officer, along with a great aunt, came to collect her to take her to her maternal grandfather's home in Birmingham. Apparently as he was next of kin, he had applied to have her. She was taken back to Birmingham, causing much heartbreak for Aunt Til and Uncle Jim. It also broke Doreen's heart to leave them, and the beautiful countryside, to live in industrial Birmingham. She cannot remember how long she lived with her grandfather and being pushed between various aunts of her mothers. She was staying at Aunt Violet's when suddenly, out of the blue, again a children's officer arrived and took her to the other side of Birmingham, just in the clothes she was wearing, to a couple to be fostered.

She went to a house, where the man was quite nice but the woman was evil. Doreen was nothing but a drudge. She would be locked under the stairs and have things thrown at her by the woman. She would get up early in the morning and take the woman her breakfast, in bed. Doreen did all the housework, washing, ironing and shopping. She never knew what it was to sit at the dining table to have a meal; she had to get herself something. Doreen said that her life was a nightmare. I do wonder what kind of vetting was done on these people to allow them to foster, but then, perhaps the woman was on her best behaviour.

One Friday afternoon coming from school, she was 16 years of age at the time, she decided that she could not put up with this kind of life any more. She would go back to Moira to be with Aunt Til and Uncle Jim. On the Saturday morning she went to the coach station and got on the bus to Moira, but she did not have any money, so the conductor took her off the bus and into the Inspector's Office. They called the police and Doreen was taken back to where she lived and was branded 'a runaway'. She had really made up her mind to get to Moira, so she ran errands for people and saved the money that she earned. Again she ran away and did eventually get to Moira, when she got to the cottage she said to Aunt Til and Uncle Jim 'I've come home, please don't send me back'. Sometime later in the day a children's officer, a policeman and her awful guardian arrived and took her back to Birmingham. Children were then under the jurisdiction of the children's officer until they were 21 years of age.

When Doreen was 18 years of age her guardians sold up, and they emigrated to Australia, abandoning her. Before they went they put her into lodgings. At this time she was earning £2.50p and her board was £2.00 a week, leaving her with a meagre amount of 50 pence to buy any essentials. All this time she was planning to go back to Moira where she did frequently visit Aunt Til and Uncle Jim. She was so unhappy living in lodgings. At the time she had a boyfriend who suggested they got married, which they did and later had a son and a daughter. So she never did get to live in Moira permanently. After 18 months Doreen's guardians returned from Australia, the man died not long after their return and later the women went into a home. I hope they treated her better than she had treated Doreen.

Doreen continued to visit Aunt Til and Uncle Jim until their deaths. They did have a daughter of their own in middle age and called her Doreen. You see Doreen was the daughter of their youth. They are very much like sisters and see each other to this day. A long time passed and Doreen was told that Uncle Jim had gone to court in the hope of keeping her, but this was impossible as her grandfather was next of kin and obviously would not sanction it.

When she was about 19 years of age, she asked the children's officer if she knew where her two sisters were. She and Mary were re-united and have a good relationship although, of course, they had missed out on their childhood years together. It was not until the 1970s that Doreen saw an advert in the paper asking if anyone knew of her whereabouts. It was Florrie and although they made contact they are not close, with all the years that had been lost, it made for a difficult relationship.

Doreen knew that to get on in this world she needed a good education and worked hard. She became a civilian secretary for the assistant Chief Constable for Crime, of the West Midlands Police. She was very much involved in the work concerning the bombings in Birmingham by the IRA. This must have brought back memories. So you see if you work hard you can achieve anything.

Unfortunately, Doreen's son died aged 30 from a brain tumour, leaving three little girls. It seems ironical that her father was the same age when he was killed and left three little girls.

This is a remarkable and sad story. It really brings home to you what it was like for families during the war. How dreadful mothers must have felt, parting with their children when they were evacuated, wondering who was going to look after them and whether they were happy. What did the young children feel being away from their families and going to a strange place to live with total strangers? It must have been awful for everyone. Families were torn apart and relationships broken, never to be reformed.

Doreen has lived in Coventry for several years. She is still waiting for her mother to fetch her as she had promised all those years ago.

Thank you Doreen, a lovely lady, for allowing me to interview you and share your memories of such a sad story. It really made me think.

Angela Atkin

Interviewed November 2006.

We'll Eat Again
Don't Know What Don't Know When

With the austerity and rationing in the war, it must have been difficult for women to cope with making meals, particularly with the meagre rations of eggs, meat and butter. Amazingly, the health of the people was good during the war years. Infant mortality declined and the average age of death from natural causes increased. Perhaps this was because rationing introduced more protein and vitamins into the diet.

The Ministry of Food started publishing 'Food Facts' Sheets in 1940, to encourage people to make the most of what they had. School meals became compulsory during war years to ensure that school children had the benefit of a main meal. We must not forget that the majority of mothers were working long hours for the war effort. There was also an early morning programme on the wireless called Kitchen Front, when recipes were passed on to the listeners.

Many home economists drove small mobile vans and touring caravans and parked them at convenient spots and demonstrated how to make the best use of rations, along with vegetables and fruit. One home economist along with a helper did her demonstration in a market square. She set up her stall and started to cook and show shoppers how to make ends meet. This was all right but the market stallholders, who were selling fruit and vegetables, were shouting out the price of their produce and drowned the ladies trying to do their demonstration. The ladies soon learnt how to shout up.

When The Women's Land Army applied for extra rations, they were told that they could have Lord Woolton's Pies; named after the Minister of Food they were not on ration. After the Land Girls had tried them once or twice they decided that they would rather do without. After reading the recipe I think that I would too. They did not appear to be appetizing. The Girls obviously wanted something more substantial as they were doing heavy labouring on the farms. The pies were made using a variety of vegetables, vegetable extract and rolled oats or oatmeal was added to the vegetable liquid. The mixture was cooked until it thickened, then poured over the vegetables then topped with potato pastry or mashed potato covered with grated cheese. The pie was served with thick brown gravy. What would Jamie Oliver think of this? One of the tips for making pastry was not to use too much fat, but to include potatoes and oatmeal, to give a change of flavour (I bet it did!). These foods were home grown and saved shipping space.

29

Oatmeal was used in a lot of recipes. Three reasons were given to encourage people to eat it. Firstly for fitness, secondly it was home produced and thirdly it was economical. Oatmeal was supposed to give you energy, help to protect against illness, make your bones strong and gave you healthy blood. Believe this if you like! Recently oats have been found to be very good for the heart.

One level tablespoon of dried egg powder, with two tablespoons of water was the equivalent of a fresh egg. Women also bottled fruit, salted beans and made chutney and pickle. The best use was made of every available ingredient.

During my research I found many peculiar fillings for sandwiches. How about this in your sandwich? Cooked mashed potato, yeast extract presumably this would be Marmite or Bovril, and chopped parsley. I think I would rather have gone hungry! Other fillings were brawn, shredded swede and chutney, (sounds delightful!) and also American sausage meat and watercress. Oh! No Marks and Spencer sandwiches then!

There were also recipes for supper dishes. How about Potato Rarebit? Using mashed potatoes as a basis for a rarebit, the potatoes were beaten until soft and smooth and like thick cream, as much grated cheese as could be spared and seasoning to taste. Spread the ingredients on hot toast and brown under the grill. Then there was Farmhouse Scramble this was comprised of margarine, grated mixed raw vegetables, two eggs or dried egg, salt and pepper. The margarine was melted in a small pan then the vegetables were added and heated until they were lightly cooked. The eggs were beaten adding salt and pepper and then poured over the vegetables, scrambled and served with potatoes. It was suggested that this could also be used as a sandwich filling or even on hot toast. Mock Duck, this sounded very posh, it is a pity that it was minus the duck, but sausage meat was used, along with cooking apples, onions and sage. Before it was put into the oven, the recipe states that the top layer should be shaped to look like a duck as much as possible. You cannot kid the people all of the time!

I have seen photographs of weddings during the war years and there was always a cake. It made me wonder how they obtained all the ingredients on such frugal rations. Well, here is the trick, the cake was not made of dried fruit, but was normally a sponge. A cardboard model would be made, in the shape of a traditional wedding cake, and placed over the sponge to make it look really good. The model would not be removed until it was time to cut the cake. Oh! What a surprise!

There is no doubt that women did have a struggle to make reasonable meals and rationing was still in force after the war. Remember there were no 'ready-meals' or 'Take-aways' then. We do not know how lucky we are now. Homes did not have freezers, all that was available was a pantry which had a thrawl (usually a paving slab). These pantries were usually on the outside wall of the house and the thrawl kept the food cool. A meat-safe was often kept in the pantry, which had a wire mesh door to keep the flies away. The window of the pantry was often covered in mesh as well.

During my research I found the following that I thought quite amusing:-

Once upon a time there were five housewives
There names were Lady Peel-Potatoes,
The Hon. Mrs. Waste-Fuel,
Miss Pour-the-Vegetable-Water-down the sink
And Mrs. Won't Eat-Carrots.
Don't let one of them put a nose in your kitchen.

Another little ditty for you:-
I saw three ships a-sailing
But not with food for me
For I am eating home-grown foods
To beat the enemy
And ships are filled with guns instead
To bring us Victory.

Angela Atkin

Bibliography
Collection of Recipes from the War Years   -   Marguerite Patten

Freda Nicholson (nee Brewer)

Some children must have viewed the prospect of evacuation with confusion or trepidation, but for six-year old Freda it was like a holiday. When the bombing started in Coventry at the end of August 1940, her parents decided that for the safety of the children mother, Freda and two-year old Roger would go and stay with Aunt Cicily and Uncle Harry Bond in Belton-in-Rutland, a small village near Rutland Water. Freda's father was in a reserved occupation, as a groom with the Co-op dairy in Swan Lane, so he was unable to accompany the family. They were living at Fir Tree Avenue, Lime Tree Park, where Freda and her brother were born. Their Grandma and Grandpa Brewer lived just down the road, the first family to move in when the road, originally called Grove Avenue, was built. If a property became vacant or partially vacant during the war, the government compelled the owner to rent it out or take in lodgers. Freda's father lodged with his mother, when he was not staying overnight at the stables, and rented out the family home. He devoted most of his time to caring for the horses in his charge. With insufficient stabling, he took a string of horses to Wolvey in the evening and fetched them again in the morning. Like many men who did not go off to war, he took part in fire-watching activities, in his case at the stables. As the bombing grew worse milk was delivered to shops, and individual customers picked it up from there, as movement was restricted by damage to the roads.

Belton-in-Rutland was very familiar to all the family as Freda's mother was born at Launde Abbey, in the nearby village of Loddington, where her father was head gardener. Freda's aunt and uncle ran the bakery in the village, although by 1940 they had retired to a cottage in the village called 'Hursley' and rented the bakery to Fred Wadd. Even then it was still the custom for some of the villagers to take their Sunday joint and Yorkshire pudding to be cooked in the bake house oven. The family stayed at 'Hursley' initially, but as it was very crowded they rented rooms with the Baptist minister, Mr Tom Wadd. The house was called 'Homeleigh' and when they first took up residence it was bounded by railings at the front, which were unfortunately sacrificed to the war effort. He too, was forced to take in lodgers when his daughter and son went into the armed forces, but the arrangement worked very well. They occupied one side of the house and Mr Wadd, a widower, had the other, with shared kitchen and toilet facilities. It was difficult for their mother as she had to go into Mr Wadd's side to the kitchen, but they all seem to have got along well. Rather than bother Mr Wadd she often went across to the village pump over the road for water.

It was a very close community and everyone knew each other. It was virtually self-sufficient with a bakery, a haberdashery run by Mrs Miller, who seemed to stock everything except food and always wore a tall hat (like the Diddymen). There was a grocers called Grococks, which supplied all their food needs and paraffin, which had to be brought through the shop to the customers, and a Post Office. There was a butcher's shop attached to the Black Horse pub and another hostelry called the Sun Inn. Pies were brought from Melton Mowbray each week and sold from a van. Freda's mother always bought a pork pie, but Freda and her friends bought the smaller boat-shaped meat pies at sixpence each, which were delicious. Newspapers were delivered by the Bradshaw brothers, who had to collect the papers from the station at East Norton, which entailed a long walk there and back. Ellis and Everard, a well-known local firm, delivered coal to the village. Their spiritual needs were served by the village church and the Baptist chapel.

Most people grew vegetables in their gardens and there was a market garden and farms surrounding the village. Italian prisoners of war were deployed on the land as the local men went off to war. They were recognised by their brown uniforms with a circular patch sewn on them. The children called them 'The Patches,' but never felt threatened by them in any way. They were billeted at Jelly's farm or at Captain Fairhurst's at Allexton. His large house was requisitioned by the military authorities and protected by barbed wire.

Freda soon settled into village life and made many friends, especially Margaret Bradshaw, a local girl and Edith Nash, an evacuee from London. When the evacuees arrived, with their gas masks and labels, they

Freda Nicholson and brother Roger

33

looked bewildered by the sudden uprooting from their homes in London to a small village in Rutland. The WVS organised the operation and villagers chose the children they wanted. Larger families such as Edith's were split up and allocated to different homes. These children came alone without a teacher or as part of a school evacuation. Most settled down very quickly, but one of Edith's brothers who was quite a bit older than the others, soon went back to London. They were absorbed into the life of the village and treated no differently from the other children. Some were made to do jobs on the farms before and after school, but no doubt the farmer's own children would be expected to contribute also.

Freda and Margaret were keen to make a vegetable patch of their own after listening to a broadcast on the radio about 'Dig for Victory.' They commandeered a plot in the back lane at the side of Margaret's house and collected bricks to make an edging and divided it into two sections. It measured about one square yard each where they grew lettuces, cress and radishes. Unfortunately Mr Davies' cows were driven back from milking along that lane and the girls often found a hoof print in the middle of their salad crop. They put up a notice saying, 'COWS KEEP OFF' just as if the animals could read. It was really a reminder to the farmer to keep his cows away. They were always ready to help out with jobs for neighbours and worked very hard one day weeding the garden of Miss Turner, for which they were paid the princely sum of two shillings and sixpence. I doubt that they received much payment when they stood in for Margaret's brothers on the newspaper deliveries, even though it was an onerous task.

Rabbits were abundant in the fields surrounding the village and men came from the town and cities nearby to shoot at weekends. One pair that Freda particularly remembers, they nicknamed Baggy and Tight. This was brought about by their choice of trousers, one wore plus-fours and the other a straight-cut style. The children never knew their correct names, but often saw Baggy and Tight walking along the street with guns over their arms. It was a habit in Freda's family to give nicknames to people and they always knew who it referred to.

Freda often went to play with a girl called Mary White as her father was a groom for Captain Watt, who kept many horses and dogs. Perhaps, because her father always worked with horses they held a great attraction for Freda, who loved both them and dogs. Sometimes they were allowed to ride the hunters back to the stables, under Mr White's supervision, although they were quite large horses. Later they would feed the dogs with Spillers Shapes, the coloured biscuits so well known at the time. There were spaniels, retrievers and terriers and it was a common sight to see Captain Watt taking

34

them for a walk through the village. He also kept chickens and turkeys at the farm, with a huge male turkey that protected the rest of the flock. One day Freda and Mary went to feed the horses, when they were caught out by 'The Big Gobbler' as they nicknamed him. He was a great guardian of his patch and rushed at them squawking and gobbling with his red wattle flying. They had to rush into the hen house to escape and were trapped there until rescued some time later.

In the summer one of the highlights of village life was the Garden Party held annually in Captain Watt's lovely large garden. Freda won a necklace one year on the 'Spinning Jenny,' a wheel that was spun and if the arrow pointed to a prize on the edge when it stopped, you were a lucky winner. Freda still treasurers that necklace to this day. Another great occasion was Harvest Festival, always a time for celebration in the farming year, when the harvest was successfully completed.

Many of the games and activities that Freda and her friends played were quite dangerous and she often wonders how she survived. She and Margaret would borrow their brothers' pushchairs and using them as go-karts speed down the hill. Another game they played at the millrace, involved walking along the top of the weir as the water rushed over. Not all their games were dangerous, they played houses in a grove of trees on the edge of the village for hours in the summer and walked miles without fear of being run over or accosted. They also helped the farmers at haymaking and harvest time by gleaning the fields after the crop was harvested. They went potato-picking or took potatoes out of the clamp and in autumn collected blackberries for pies and jam-making and rosehips for rosehip syrup. Freda and Margaret had a favourite rose bush in the churchyard, which they considered the best in the village, but kept the knowledge to themselves. The children collected nettles, which were hung in bags in the bicycle shed to dry. Why they did this Freda is not sure, but maybe it was for winter feed for the animals. On Oak Apple Day, 29th May, it was the custom to wear a bunch of oak leaves, if not the lads of the village would brush your legs with stinging nettles. A painful experience I should imagine.

All the children in the village attended the local school until they reached the age of eleven, when they went on to the senior school in Uppingham or the grammar school in Oakham. The evacuees were treated exactly the same as the local children. The school consisted of two rooms, one for infants under the care of Mrs Turnbull and one for juniors under Mrs Ringrose. The classrooms were heated in winter by a pot-belly stove, on which was heated water to make Bovril drinks for the children during cold weather. Everyone lived locally including the teachers, so they all went home for dinner. The teaching concentrated on reading, writing, arithmetic and nature. They had to work on slates most of the time, as there was a chronic shortage of paper. There was a great emphasis on nature, after all it surrounded them and most of the inhabitants of a village like Belton would spend their lives on the land in some way or other. The children were taken for nature walks and returned to school to press the flowers they had collected and discuss what they had seen. It was the place where Freda learned her sewing skills too. She believes that she had a better education there than she might have received in a city, although her handwriting has suffered by not developing free handwriting at an earlier stage, however, she is great at writing in capital letters.

The children also attended Sunday school at the Baptist chapel where Mr Wadd was the minister. They were taught by Cathy Browett who delivered milk to the village. Freda often went to collect the eggs with Cathy and help her. Not only did Freda and her friends attend the Baptist Sunday school, but they also joined the Anglican Sunday school with the object of being included in their Christmas party. She joined the local Brownie pack too, which met at the vicarage.

During the four years that Freda spent in the village she never felt homesick, because it was like a second home to her. She missed her father, but he visited on some Sundays when he could, the first time putting his bicycle on the train to Tugby Station and cycling from there to Belton. It was quite a distance and his return trip was made in the dark, without the aid of street-lights. After that he came on the bus and went home loaded down with rabbits, eggs and mushrooms, for food was hard to come by in Coventry. Freda first experienced fear for her father when the November 1940 blitz happened. News spread that Coventry was on fire and Freda cried, 'My daddy's there.' They could see the glow in the sky as the city burned, even at that distance. It was four days before he was able to get a message through that he was all right. There were very few telephones in the village, but all the lines were down in Coventry anyway. It was a great relief for the family to know that he was safe.

Freda and her family had experienced bombing before they left Coventry for Belton, so they were familiar with some aspects of war. When a barrage balloon was towed over the village everyone came out to look at it, as it was such a novelty. No doubt the evacuees were also accustomed to such sights, but the locals were fascinated by it. However, when they experienced bombs being dropped it was a great shock. On the evening of the 25th May 1942 the villagers were just settling down to supper, putting the children to bed, having a drink in the pub or doing the garden when the peace was shattered. A Dornier 217 flew low over the village being chased by two allied fighter planes. Machine guns were heard as the fighters tried to shoot down the bomber. Freda was called to the window by her mother, who had spotted the plane, but Mr Wadd rushed them under the stairs where they waited until the danger had passed. The German pilot jettisoned his bombs over the village and headed for the east coast. One of the fighter pilots was injured but the Dornier escaped. Five bombs dropped in a line through the village. Damage was done to buildings such as the butcher's shop and a barn, leaving large craters. There was a lot of cleaning up to be done in the village with tiles off roofs, windows missing and debris strewn about the streets, but they had been very lucky. Miraculously the only casualties were a cat and a rabbit.

Freda had a great desire to be a Land Girl during the war, partly because of her love of animals and the environment and partly because she admired the uniform. One day a young woman stepped off the bus that terminated opposite Mr Wadd's house, dressed as a Land Girl. She looked confused and lost, so Freda's mother asked her in for a cup of tea. When she said to which farm she was allocated, Freda's mother said, 'I wouldn't work for him.' She persuaded her to find an alternative farm and she went to work for Captain Fairhurst instead. The girl's name was also Freda, so maybe this was an incentive to Mrs Brewer to advise against a billet that she thought would not be suitable.

It was always a source of interest to have the bus terminus right opposite their house. If the children were not at school the bus driver allowed Freda and her friends to play on the bus while he went into the pub opposite for a break. They did no harm and played happily until he returned. Sometimes he bought them Vimto and Smith's crisps, with a twist of blue paper for the salt that so many of us remember from our childhood.

During the build-up to D-Day convoys of lorries, jeeps and other military vehicles passed by the end of the village, driven by American servicemen. These convoys were patrolled by military police, but it did not stop the servicemen from chatting to the children who were watching them with interest. They threw bags of boiled sweets to the children, which was a great treat. Some of the boys took advantage of their generosity and dodged to the other side of the village to catch the convoy for a second helping.

Freda's uncle played the organ at the church in the village of Allexton. He employed Margaret to pump the organ for him and she did the job very well. However, if she was unable to do it, Freda was expected to stand in for her friend. Not being so enthusiastic as Margaret, she would lose concentration and stop pumping up the pressure. The organ could not perform properly and her uncle became exasperated, calling to Freda in her place behind the organ, 'Freda, will you do the job properly.' She cannot remember ever being paid for her efforts, maybe that was why her performance was less than perfect.

The family had some difficulty regaining possession of their home in Fir Tree Avenue as the tenants were reluctant to move out. This delayed their return to Coventry until later in 1944. Freda remembers walking up the garden path for the first time in many years and a large dog bounding towards them which ran out of the gate, but they let it go. Changes had taken place in their absence and they had to get used to more restrictions in their life. The tar-pots that were placed intermittently along Broad Lane to create thick black smoke to camouflage the factories in Banner Lane still existed. There were shelters built outside their house to accommodate two families, looking like garages with doors facing each other. All the military vehicles that had covered one side of Fletchamstead Highway for months early in the year, in preparation for the D-Day offensive, had gone by the time they returned.

Freda returned to Whoberley School in Tile Hill Lane, where she had begun her schooling in 1939. In those early days as an infant pupil she attended school on a part-time basis, mornings one week and afternoon the next. When war began the children had to carry their gas-masks in their cardboard boxes wherever they went. Air-raid drill was practiced and the children filed into the shelter, a tunnel under the playing fields. She hated going into the tunnel and is sure that it is the cause of the claustrophobia she has suffered from ever since. Freda went into the junior school when she returned and the following year went up into the senior school. All departments were contained within the same establishment. She resumed her friendship with Barbara Fearn, Maureen Hughes and Brenda Stagg, girls she had known before she went to Belton. These friends remained together until they left school at the age of fifteen and meet up annually for a reunion. Friends have always been important to Freda and she still keeps in touch with Margaret and Edith with whom she spent so many happy times as an evacuee in Belton.

Lynn Hockton

Interviewed August 2006

Irene Chainey

During the war Irene was living with her parents in Gulson Road, Coventry. She worked as a shorthand typist in the Aeroplane Drawing Office at Armstrong Whitworth Aircraft Limited at Whitley Aerodrome. Her boyfriend, Bob, also worked for the same company, although he was based at Baginton Aerodrome.

She lived in Coventry throughout the war, and has many memories of the city at that time. She remembers the house being 'blacked out' at night either with shutters, curtains made from blackout material or anything to exclude the light at night. How even the vehicles had to be fitted with special shades so that the light from the headlights could not be seen. However, with the rationing of petrol there tended to be fewer vehicles on the roads during the night. Even the signposts were taken down, so that they would not help the enemy if the country were invaded.

Irene still remembers the sirens going off. Many people have asked her over the years since, how she felt on hearing the sirens, and whether she was frightened. She and her family heard so many cases of people who were killed, but also many of people who were saved too. It felt like the saying the soldiers had during the First World War, that if it had your name on it, then that was that. Towards the start of the war one of Irene's friends went to the cinema with her boyfriend. Whilst they were there the sirens began to sound. They had the choice of whether to stay at the cinema and hope it was spared any damage or go home. There was an element of risk whatever they decided to do. They decided to make for home and take the chance. On their way home they were both killed, whereas if they had made the choice to stay in the cinema they would have been safe. It still makes her think of how one decision can have such consequences.

Irene's father was a Master Printer by trade and even with the shortage of paper he still maintained a small printing workshop at the back of the house. On the night of 21st October 1940 the air raid siren went off, just as they were getting ready for bed. They sheltered under the stairs listening to the noise of an aircraft getting louder as it prepared to drop its bombs. They heard the aircraft drop a stick of five bombs, each one getting closer. After her father had heard the fourth one he said, 'This one is ours,' and so it turned out. Although it was technically, and fortunately for them, a small bomb the explosion was tremendous. It dropped between the house and the workshop. As the noise subsided they could hear the slates falling off the roof and splashing down into the soft-water tank. Her father's workshop was totally destroyed, and she still has a photograph of her mother holding the cat, standing outside the rubble that was the workshop.

That night an Air-Raid Warden took them to a nearby surface shelter where they stayed until morning. They went back to look at the house, but there was no possibility of them living there, as in addition to the damage caused by the bomb, there was no water, gas or electricity. They salvaged what they could from their home.

Irene's boyfriend, Bob, had heard from a friend that a bomb had dropped near them and cycled over to see if they were safe and found them looking at the wreckage of their house. Irene's new bicycle, which had been left in her father's workshop for safekeeping had a huge slab of concrete hanging over it. Bob decided that he would be able to rescue it. Despite her protests about the danger, Bob scrambled over the bricks and rubble and retrieved it. She remembers being hugely grateful, both that he was safe and that he had rescued her bicycle, as having transport in those days was everything. A large piece of shrapnel from the bomb had gone right through the metal

Irene and Bob Chainey

frame under the saddle, but it was still useable. In fact she rode that bicycle throughout the war and for many years afterwards.

As they were not able to live in their house, they went to stay with her aunt and uncle in Earlsdon. They were not the only ones to be taken in by this generous couple for they were already accommodating Irene's cousin, aunt and uncle who had also been bombed out. They had lost their house and their shop, their home and their livelihood too. On the night of the November blitz on Coventry her family was already homeless, sharing the house in Earlsdon with five other people. They were very grateful for a place to stay and did not worry about the lack of space.

Everyone worked so hard to keep things going. Later on in the war Bob was working so many hours, sometimes working shifts around the clock. Once he worked an entire weekend, both day and night. Eventually, exhausted he went home to sleep at his parents' house. That evening the air raid sirens went off as bombs were dropping near the house. After trying in vain to wake Bob, his family all retreated to the Anderson shelter at the bottom of the garden. The raid lasted throughout the night until the 'All Clear' sounded in the morning. At the sound of the 'All Clear' Bob woke and went downstairs, to meet his family coming out of the shelter, and asked if there had been an air raid. They still laugh at this story, for there cannot be many people who have slept through an all night air raid.

Irene still lives in Coventry, with Bob whom she married in 1943. They are both very active members of Coventry Cathedral.

Ali McGarry

Thank you to Irene and Bob Chainey for their memories of the war. Interviewed summer 2006

Iris Downham (formerly Webster)

By the time war was declared on Germany in 1939, Daimler's shadow factory at Allesley was already in full production making Hercules aircraft engines for the war effort. In truth the works was making one half of the engine, the other half was made by Standard at Banner Lane.

The hum of production lines as the factory worked round the clock dominated this once rural community. Residents of Brown's Lane, families like the Websters, suddenly found themselves thrust into the front line of war.

Iris and Derek Webster were living at bungalow 292, just a stone's throw from the main factory gate. 'It belonged to Derek's parents,' said Iris.

'With the ever present possibility of the Daimler being bombed Derek sandbagged around the back bedroom,' she recalled, 'but ironically it was my parent's house, number 46 at the other end of Brown's Lane, that was hit by a stray bomb. The house was declared unsafe and they moved with my sister Molly to live with us at 292.'

When Iris and Derek's first baby a son John, was born in July 1940, Iris was offered accommodation in the Cotswold village of Ilmington. So in September she and John left Allesley leaving Derek at the bungalow. Derek's day job was working at the Daimler on maintenance. He was one of four men who looked after the structure of the factory. His war job was a despatch rider in the Home Guard, and he took advantage of the motorbike to ride over to Ilmington for weekends with Iris and John.

Iris remembers that in the November, the night after the Coventry Blitz, Derek rode all round Coventry looking up friends and relatives and then made for Ilmington where he collapsed on the bed, sleeping a good twenty four hours.

In April 1941 Iris and John returned to Brown's Lane with the air raids still taking place. The city was making a huge contribution to the war effort making aero engines, complete aircraft and military vehicles, and night attacks by the Luftwaffe were a constant threat.

'We often found ourselves adopting a rather unusual practice of providing floor space for neighbours who brought anything they could find to roll up in,' Iris said. 'You never knew who would be with you for breakfast.'

'Several nights we heard the thud of bombs and waited to see how many houses had been hit. On one night approximately half the production line at Daimler was destroyed along with many neighbouring houses. Fortunately for the occupants it was normal for most of Brown's Lane to trundle out to Corley where locals were more than happy to provide beds for the night.

Consequently most of the houses in Brown's Lane stood empty at night and Jim Stevens, a special constable with Warwickshire Constabulary, would be out on his rounds checking that all was well.'

Then in 1942 Derek volunteered and joined the RAF. He was stationed in Lincolnshire and on one occasion when he had a thirty-six hour pass, Iris and John made the journey from Coventry Station to Skegness.

'How I managed the journey with all the luggage and a small child I shall never know,' Iris recalled. 'We had to travel to Nuneaton and change trains. I struggled over the bridge with a heavy case and John, who kept dropping his Home Guard knitted doll. It was his most precious possession and we couldn't leave it behind. I screamed as I saw the train begin to pull out of the station but luckily the stationmaster heard me and stopped the train. We left at teatime so were travelling in the dark. It was a steam engine of course with sparks and smuts flying past the window. When we arrived at Skegness I had to find my own way to the bed and breakfast small terraced house where a room had been booked. Derek joined us there but had to leave in the early hours to return to camp before his pass ran out.

He worked on maintaining gliders in a team of twenty men as ground staff. They were always in great demand and Derek put his woodworking skills to good use while stretching fabric onto the wings and fuselage. After the overhaul and repairs the gliders were always flown by these men to test their safety.'

At home in Allesley life continued as usual with a growing community spirit in the village and Brown's Lane. While pre-war activities like the operatic productions ceased other organisations carried on their meetings.

'You could almost tell the seasons of the year by the events that were held in the Parish Room: like the annual New Year's Eve party, a themed Easter dance and Christmas bazaar. However, when the Parish Room became a decontamination centre many activities ceased and the guides and scouts no longer had a meeting place.'

'Not surprisingly the Women's Institute which I belonged to continued meeting. A room in the Old Rectory was often used. At other times committee members met at Arden House, the home of Dr Margaret Mitchell, and for our monthly meeting members would go to the Stone House,'

'At the start of the war the Church of England School opposite the Parish Room became a first aid station. Just three years before it had been transferred to the Local Education Authority by the Rector of Allesley, the Rev.Winser.'

'Older pupils were sent to Southbank Road School on a voluntary basis at the end of 1939, and juniors went to Brownshill Green Chapel. A year later the village school re-opened for nine to fourteen year olds.'

Early in the war food was in short supply and the Blitz had brought an end to shopping, as locals had known it. Dig for Victory was the order of the day and Allesley people responded with vigour.

'We used the back garden for growing vegetables like all the other households, with Jim Stevens giving us cabbage plants from his allotment,' said Iris. 'We were luckier than those who lived in the centre of town as we had several local shops and of course the farms where some food was available. On Wednesdays we walked to Mr Tuckey the butcher at the crossroads of Butt Lane and Brown's Lane to buy offal with our ration book. Meat was in short supply so occasionally as a treat we would be offered a rabbit or chicken already prepared by Mr Tuckey.'

'At the top of Hawkesmill Lane was Southall's farm where I would go for fish. Mrs Southall would let me know when the fish was in and I would scrub the pram out, put a plastic sheet in the well at the bottom, place boards across, sit John in and go to collect fish for everyone. I can see Mrs Southall now in her sacking apron. With the fish wrapped up in the plastic sheet, the boards in place and John sitting on top, we made the long push home. It was quite an experience walking to the farm as they belonged to the old village and we in Brown's Lane were considered living in the new village.'

'We had some cold winters but no central heating. The fuel came from Dockers the coal merchants for our open fire. We cooked on an old gas stove and used a black enamel kettle on the stove for boiling water. We also had paraffin heaters and lamps.'

'Although tea was rationed we looked forward to the food parcel from my pen friend Helen in America. We always shared the packets of tea with neighbours. Four packets of tea had to go a long way.'

'Occasionally we would go into Coventry by bus. The number 10, a 14-seater, would pick up passengers along Brown's Lane and make the journey to town via Butt Lane, Butcher's Lane and Allesley Old Road. It was a real social occasion as we picked up friends and neighbours in the village. By the time we reached Allesley Old Road the bus was full but somehow everyone squeezed on with their large shopping baskets. However, we were lucky to have the choice of two buses as the number 7, a 30-seater, started from Woods Cottage at the top of Windmill Hill. This bus took the more direct route into town by the Holyhead Road. Incidentally there were no designated bus stops. Amazingly a passenger would probably shout – driver, can you stop at the house with the green curtains?'

'Of course many of the shops in town no longer existed after the air raids, but luckily we had Woolworths in the City Arcade, a few little shops leading down to the Barracks Market where many traders would set up twice a week. We would walk down to Pool Meadow hoping to get a seat on the little bus for the return journey.'

'Occasionally I would walk the pram into town, a good three miles, but we had rather an unusual arrangement with neighbours. If one of them caught the bus to town they would walk the pram back from a pre-arranged shop and I could catch the bus. That's pram sharing rather than car sharing!'

Iris found part-time work at the GEC on the village side of the Daimler factory.

'I worked in accounts for Reg Walters in the wages department. Fortunately my mother stayed at home with John.'

'On the social side the Daimler were very generous and gave fancy dress parties for the children. My mother made several costumes both for John and neighbours' children.'

'Despite the horrors of war we made the best of things and that brought the community together like never before.'

Elizabeth Draper

Many thanks to Iris for her wartime memories.
Interviewed November 2006

Village Life in Wartime

Margaret was born in Coventry and lived near Gulson Road, in a two-bedroomed terraced house, with her parents and two brothers. She attended All Saints School and her first memory is of the Head Teacher heating the milk on winter days and making Horlicks for the children. By the start of the war she was in the junior school where they were issued with gas masks that had a very rubbery smell, which had to be carried everywhere. Each box contained a bar of chocolate, but this must have been only in her school as it was not a usual extra.

When the house was completely destroyed by a bomb the family had to be evacuated. The first move was to a house just outside Kenilworth, but after an air raid, when that town was bombed, Margaret's parents thought it better to move further away. The property they lived in had no air raid shelter and they had felt very vulnerable. They then moved to Cubbington; the Domesday survey reported the village as 'situated in a small hollow.'

Fortunately Margaret's mother had an old aunt, Emily, living in the village and she found the family accommodation. This was an old cottage, in a block of two placed back to back in a courtyard behind the houses in New Street, a small lane near to the church and leading up to Cubbington woods. The cottage was built of sandstone and had a slate roof. A path of uneven bricks lay in front of the cottage, but did not reach the lane. There was a very small garden. Before the war the cottage had been condemned so the local people had taken the opportunity to help themselves to any useful items they could. Anything wooden such as the picture rails, mantelpiece and staircase rails had been removed. Fortunately the stairs were still there. The cottage was very tiny and the family of five had to fit into it and make the best of it. However, the family were glad enough of anything to escape the bombing.

Sadly, while living in Cubbington, Margaret's father had to be admitted to hospital terminally ill and died there. Following a tooth extraction her brother, aged sixteen, contracted a heart infection from which he too, died.

The one downstairs room contained a recess, which had to serve as a pantry. A meat-safe sat on a shelf and its door had a fine metal grill to keep out flies. A milk jug was covered with a muslin cloth, weighted with beads for the same purpose. All food items had to be kept in the 'pantry.' There was no sink or drain and a bucket was kept for waste water. A big jug was kept to carry fresh water from a communal pump in the yard.

For cooking there was a big, black, iron range, which needed black-leading regularly to keep it free from rust. To economise on coal, a brick was placed either side of the fire and a container was placed underneath the fire to catch the ashes. There was a hob on each side of the fire to put a kettle or pan on and beneath one hob was an oven. At floor level there was a fender and inside this was a companion set which held a brush, small shovel and a poker. There was also a coal-scuttle and a toasting fork. Newspaper was folded into plaits and Margaret's mother chopped wood to get the fire going. To help it draw she would hold an open newspaper across the space. There was a fireguard to prevent sparks, from the coal, spitting out.

The aunt had managed to acquire some furniture, all second hand, but appreciated nevertheless. The downstairs room was furnished with a sideboard, four hard chairs, a sofa and a scrubbed wooden table. This was covered with a chenille cloth when not in use, which was not often. Everything had to be done on the table from washing oneself to preparing the vegetables.

Only the houses in the main street had gas connected, so the cottage had to be lit by a paraffin oil lamp. This stood on the scrubbed table and if the wick was not trimmed frequently, the lamp smelled and smoked a lot, leaving a black mark on the low ceiling. There was a necessity for fly papers to hang from the ceiling. As they were sticky Margaret did not appreciate getting her hair caught on them.

The family also had an old wireless that had a heavy accumulator, containing an acid, which had to be charged up at intervals. There was also a wind-up gramophone, which had to be stuffed with old socks to keep its noise down. The floor's uneven blue bricks were covered with rag rugs. The front door had a big blanket hung on a wire and a sausage along the bottom to keep out the draughts. Blackout curtains hung at all the cottage windows.

Upstairs a curved staircase led to the two bedrooms where cocoa-tin lids had to be nailed over the holes in the floorboards. One room was large enough for a double and single bed, but the other only had space for a single; this room had no window. There was no space for other furniture so clothes were stored in suitcases under the beds or hung on the backs of the doors. On the floors were small home-made rag rugs. In the winter the family went to bed with a torch for light, a stone hot water bottle or a plate out of the oven covered with a cloth gave some warmth.

From a nail, on the wall by the back door, hung a galvanised bath. This was brought inside once a week so that the family could bathe in front of the fire. This involved a lot of work boiling enough water for a decent bath. *'Friday Night is Amami Night'* (This was a jingle advertising the shampoo).

There was a water butt and the soft water was used for hair washing followed by rinsing, in a weak vinegar solution, to make it shine. Margaret had short hair tied with a ribbon, but if she went out for a special occasion her mother would put 'Dinky Curlers' in or use curling tongs. She also put the hair in rags, but as Margaret says 'I don't think it was very successful because I never did resemble Shirley temple!'

Margaret admits that she did not appreciate how hard women had to work even just to heat up the water using kettles. The lavatory had a wooden seat over a bucket and had to be shared with the neighbours. Toilet paper consisted of newspapers cut into squares and hung inside. Ashes from fires made a huge heap outside the toilet and if no one came to empty the buckets a resident had to do the task. This they would do by mixing the contents with the ash and putting them into a hole in the garden.

There was a communal washhouse and each house was allotted a certain day to use it. Inside the washhouse stood a copper boiler that required filling with water, from the pump outside, and a fire lit underneath it. In the corner stood a large wooden mangle with wooden rollers, a dolly tub and a posser, used to move the washing about in the tub. Hard green soap was used along with washing soda. To make the white clothes look brighter a blue bag was put into the rinsing water. A bowl of starch was made to dip in articles that required stiffening. When the washing was done the water had to be baled out using a ladle. Washday made for a lot of hard work, but the results would be on view to all the neighbours as the clothes hung across the gardens outside. It was a very busy and energetic time for the women, taking up the whole day.

If washday turned out wet, clothes had to be put on a wooden clothes horse in front of the fire. The condensation from them made the house smell damp. Once dry the ironing had to be done on the kitchen table, which was protected by a folded blanket. Two flat irons were used after being heated on the fire.

Another full day's work was provided by the visit of the chimney sweep. On a windy day, if the wind was in the 'wrong' direction, the room would become full of smoke. There was quite a performance when the sweep came, which was frequent, as the coal was of a poor quality and made much soot. All the furniture had to be covered. The sweep put his rods through a slit in a cloth and the children would be sent outside to see the brush come out of the chimney pot. The soot was kept for spreading on the garden. Of course it was the housewife who had the job of cleaning up afterwards. To save money some of the villagers would sweep their chimneys themselves. To do this they pushed a holly branch up the chimney or swung a brick on a rope down the chimney pot. Margaret's mother would not risk doing this. When there was a chimney fire, the village children would rush out to see where the flames were coming from. They thought it was a thrilling sight

Margaret's mother planted vegetables in the small garden, lettuce, potatoes and carrots. During the war-everyone was urged to *Dig for Victory.* At the end of the small garden there was a small shed for coal. All the bags had to be carefully counted out when the coalman made a delivery. At the other side of the fence was a pigsty. That was useful for the pigs ate any waste food. Waste water was poured away at the end of the garden.

There were several occasional, but regular, visitors to the village. The doctor held a weekly surgery in the village, using the front room of Aunt Emily's cottage. To consult a doctor patients had to pay a small amount to be on his panel, but many villagers treated ailments themselves using the old fashioned remedies. A cold was treated with an inhalation of Friars Balsam in water and maybe goose grease or camphorated oil was rubbed on the chest. There were many more home treatments. Margaret was lucky she never had to see the doctor. If she complained of any ailment she was told to stop whining and go and have a ride on her bike.

A Rag and Bone man frequently arrived shouting 'Rags and Bones.' Children whose mothers could find any scrap items, such as clothes or pans, were given a balloon, or gold fish, in return. A knife grinder took a portable grinder offering to sharpen knives or scissors. Gypsies too, paid visits to the houses selling items they had made such as pegs, or offering to tell fortunes.

In the village there was a post office and general store, a butcher's, bakery and dairy, and of course rationing was in force. In those days stock was delivered to shops in bulk and food was individually weighed out for customers. Biscuits were in large tins to be sold in separate amounts, sugar weighed into blue bags, butter sold in pats and cheese cut with a wire. Sweets came in big jars. While the children were interested in different sweets most mothers could only afford the cheapest. Vinegar was in barrels and sold by the half pint. Tobacco twist and snuff were also available.

The village people were 'rough and ready,' but had hearts of gold, always there to help others when needed. It was always 'send for Aunt Emily' who assisted at childbirths, laying out the dead and also sat up all night with anyone ill. She was very bandy, due to having rickets as a child, and the children would call after her 'you couldn't stop a pig in a passage.' She was never offended, but would roar with laughter until her false teeth fell down. That caused more laughter. Aunt Emily liked her drink of stout and would take her jug to the outdoor which shocked some people.

49

There were some mentally handicapped children locally, but they were all treated kindly. One girl was extremely thin; she had a spinal disease and was wheeled in a long invalid carriage. Some of the village children used to take her out. One friend lived with two old uncles in a dirty, tumbledown cottage. There was much sympathy for her. It was thought that the council must have heard about her, for she was taken away and put in a children's home at Myton, where the hospice is now. Margaret went to visit her there and was very shocked. She said 'I had two brothers and had to be very modest, but she poor child had to stand in a queue, boys and girls with no clothes on, waiting to be bathed. I think she was about nine years old. I remember feeling very glad that I had got my mother.'

Another friend of Margaret lived in a very tumbledown cottage on a farm where her father was the cowman. Visitors had to cross three fields to get to the house. He told children that his cap got greasy because of holding his head against the cow's sides as he was doing the milking. When his hat got worn out he took it off and his dogs got to eat it. They didn't know whether to believe that. His wife made beestings pudding. It was from the first, very rich milk from the cow as soon as it had given birth to a calf. Margaret liked going there because she had a lot of fun, sliding up and down the haystacks. There was a big duck pond, which was fun for dipping in nets and also watching dragonflies, frogs, toads and moorhens nearby. The children were told never to go into the water because it was deep and dangerous.

The village school was so close that a pupil could stay at home until the bell rang, then rush into the playground and make it to the end of the line as the class marched in. Margaret was in the junior department, while her brother was in the infants. The Headmaster was the only trained teacher left owing to wartime conditions, while the other staff comprised of local women. There was one large classroom, which could be separated by sliding doors according to need. A large tortoise stove provided heat in the winter and the caretaker kept it lit. At the front of the room stood the teacher's high wooden desk and a blackboard on an easel. The children sat at small desks with bench seats for two. Other equipment was kept in large cupboards. There was a nature table displaying frogspawn, caterpillars in jars, carrot tops and cress on a flannel.

Margaret thought it would be a great honour to be a monitor. They collected the books and rubbed the chalk off the blackboard. To have been an ink monitor would have been even better, in Margaret's eyes, for they were allowed to go into the playground to mix the powdered ink and fill the inkwells. Regrettably she never did achieve that goal. She found, that writing with ink was a messy business resulting not only in blots on her work, but ink on her clothes and fingers. Her pen nibs were always becoming crossed from pressing too hard on the paper when writing.

Basic lessons were taught, but there was no special gym equipment for physical activities. When playing games a coloured band was worn across the chest to differentiate the teams. Pumps were worn and carried in a special home-made bag. Margaret enjoyed country dancing. In the spring the children danced around a maypole holding coloured ribbons that formed a pattern as the dancers wove in and out. Because of the war the children learned to 'make do and mend' at school. They learned to patch and darn, make buttonholes and knit. Margaret enjoyed crafts so was interested in making seamen's navy blue jerseys, grey woollen sea-boot stockings and balaclavas. The children were allowed to insert their name and address, inside the garment, with the chance of receiving a thank-you note in return. Perhaps this was to encourage the children to use their best handwriting.

Rosehips were collected by children living in the country, supervised by their teachers, which were used to make syrup for babies. It was also an opportunity for a nature lesson as the class walked over several fields. However, Margaret confesses she was more interested in the latest Bette Davis film than in bogweed or fungus! Visiting the cinema was not easy because the nearest cinema was in Leamington and transport was infrequent, but it did not stop the girls discussing the latest film idols.

Owing to the shortage of farm labourers the children went potato picking, a job Margaret really loved. They used to ride their bikes to a farm at Weston-under-Wetherly, carrying a bucket on the handlebars as they were allowed to bring home some potatoes. Margaret considers that she must have been a very odd child because she would find the biggest roasting . potato and hide it under a sack. She expects her mother would much rather have had a bucketful of smaller ones. They used to sit on a straw bale and sing *Don't Fence me In* or *She'll be Coming Round the Mountain*, eating their sandwiches and drinking the most awful black tea without sugar. The farmer would mark out their individual areas with a stick, but when he got to the end of the row, Margaret surreptitiously moved her sticks in a bit. No one knew why she was always finished first.

There was also a Sunday school to attend. It was held in the main school with the desks being pushed together. The children were given a little stamp to put in a book whenever they attended. One day they heard that there was a new vicar at the Methodist church. He was a young man and described by other girls as looking like a film star; he was smashing. So Margaret decided that she would go with some of her friends to view this young

Adonis. Well he had a face full of acne and buck-teeth, but he did have a nice smile. He made them sing the hymn *Jesus Wants me for a Sunbeam*. Margaret decided she didn't want to be a sunbeam and would rather stick with the vicar she knew!

There was plenty of time for leisure pursuits. Margaret joined the Girl Guides run by the vicar's daughter who appointed her as patrol leader of the Orchid Patrol. She thought it was a funny looking flower and rather wished it had been a rose or a daffodil. On one occasion she was asked to carry the flag into the church on the Guides Thinking Day. 'I remember wearing a thick leather belt round my waist for the flag to fit in.'

Margaret confesses that she was always rather naughty. Guides had to learn the rules, but the group of girls in Orchid Patrol were not remotely interested. Instead they read copies of the *Beano*; they were always nice and quiet. However, they did learn various knots and a bit of first-aid, gaining several badges. Margaret had no problem achieving her knitting badge. She clearly remembers going to the house of a Chief Guider in Leamington and having to knit a sock, including turning the heel, without a pattern. That was easy; she had done it several times before. She was also awarded a badge for housecraft. This consisted of ironing a man's handkerchief starting with the edges. She was awarded her cyclists badge after mending a puncture on a bike; this was also something she had done many times. She says she had bent many a tablespoon trying to get the tyre off the rim. She then put the inner tube into a bowl of water and watched for bubbles to reveal the hole.

The Guides also went camping and slept in bell tents, made of canvas and slept on straw palliasses. They were told not to touch the outside of the tent, as it would let in the rain. There were guy ropes to keep the tent up on a big pole and the edges had to be rolled up in the morning to air it. There was a big marquee for the food tent. It was a very big camp because there were many guides from different areas. They had a lot of fun.

During the day the guides had to pick big Victoria and yellow plums. They were put in huge boxes and they were on their honour not to eat any. Margaret says she never ate one although they looked lovely. The fruit was graded. Some for tins, others for jam or to be sold fresh. The only trouble was there were hundreds of wasps everywhere, but fortunately she was never stung. It did not help that the girls were given jam for tea! The camp was probably at Shipston on Stour and it led down to the river. There were lovely camp fires in the evening and the guides sat round singing. Margaret says that she cannot remember the washing arrangements!

Margaret had an old 'sit-up-and-beg' bike and used to ride for miles with friends, three or four abreast, taking a drink and sandwiches; they would be out all day. Otherwise they played in Cubbington woods quite a lot. Not far from the woods stood Weston Colony, at that time a secure mental hospital. The only warnings issued were that if the siren went, the children had to go straight home as it meant a patient was missing. The other warning was to not go too far as Weston Mill was a working mill and the river flowed very strongly. Two young girls had been drowned there. The children would leave their bikes by the hedge; nothing was locked.

In the spring there were plenty of wild flowers to pick, among which were violets, primroses, cowslips and bluebells. Trees produced catkins and sticky buds in turn. There was plenty of bird life to observe, such as bluetits, wrens, blackbirds and many more. Cuckoos were heard and sometimes a woodpecker pecking a hole in a tree. Lying in the fields, among all the different grasses, the youngsters watched skylarks climbing into the sky. There were lots of lovely butterflies, red admirals, peacocks and meadow browns. Rabbits and hares were occasionally seen and sometimes a small muntjac deer would appear. In the autumn it was fun to scuffle among fallen leaves and to collect blackberries, crab apples and mushrooms from the fields. Even in the winter it was interesting to see the hoar frost and snow making pretty outlines on trees and revealing the tracks of animals. On the way home wood was collected for the fire

An old aunt of Margarets kept the Post Office and General Store at Bubbenhall. If you know Bubbenhall it was right opposite the spring, which was very fast flowing from a pipe in the wall. This provided the villagers with their drinking water. It is still there, but is only a trickle now due to building work being done. Margaret used to ride to see her aunt, on her trusty bike. Her aunt was very kind and used to give her lemonade and sweets from the shop, but first she had to brave all the wasps. To trap them there were jam jars, containing jam water, hung from string round the door. The sweetness enticed the wasps, which fell into the water and thus were drowned. The aunt was often busy, using her mincing machine, in the outhouse where she used to make faggots.

'We were never bored.' Outdoor games the children played, like most children everywhere, were marbles, five-stones, whip and top and skipping with a long rope across the street. There were also ball games and singing ones. To play hopscotch, marks were chalked on the pavement. Conkers had their season, but some of the boys baked them in the oven or soaked them in vinegar. That was considered to be cheating.

If it was wet, board games, playing cards or jigsaws were brought out. French knitting was quite popular. Four nails were put into the top of a cotton reel, wool hooked over them and after a time it came out like a sausage. Little mats could be produced if the sausage was long enough. Making patterns using painted potatoes was fun, if rather messy.

Margaret's mother bought loose ends of wool from the mills, called thrums. They were offcuts from carpets, but they made a nice mat when pegged into canvas and Margaret helped her mother make them.

On dark evenings the children would play in the street where there was a dim gas lamp. The stars were clearly visible in the dark sky. There were bats flying about, and screech owls and the bark of a fox could be heard. One game played was 'Jacky, Jacky Show your Lamp.' One child would run off and flash his torch and the others would have to try and find him. One cheeky lad would climb the roofs and flash his lamp by the chimney pots. It was a wonder he did not get killed.

In the summer there was always a church fete in the village. It was held in a field next to the church and was in aid of funds for its upkeep. This was always great fun as everyone was busy for weeks beforehand getting ready for the event. The Women's Institute had a big stall where they sold knitted toys and tea-cosies, home-made pies, cakes, jam and marmalade. Margaret's mother was a member and made aprons to sell, using the tails of men's shirts. She put a frill round, all done on an old treadle sewing machine. There were also stalls selling produce from the allotments. The children's fancy dress competition was very popular. 'I remember going as a pirate and I remember my face being very sore having put brown shoe polish on it to give me a tan.'

The manager of the sawmills had a pianola so that was brought out. You could hear the music and watch the stiff rolls of paper, which had various holes in it, turn round. A friend's father played in the Cubbington Silver Band; he played a sousaphone and it was kept at home. Margaret would go to her friend's house and blow it and try to make some sounds out of it. It was an enormous instrument it curved round the body and over the shoulder.

Although the villagers were poor the harvest festival was always very well supported. The church was decorated beautifully with flowers and garden produce such as giant marrows, leeks and cabbages.

Bonfire night was great fun and preparations began a few weeks before. Wood was collected for the fire, which was held in someone's long front garden and fireworks consisted of a few sparklers. The children used to put potatoes in the ashes to roast. Although they got black from the ash they always tasted lovely.

During the winters there were always heavy snowfalls, more than we get now. Margaret loved that. 'We made long slides and snowmen and had snowball fights. We also went sledging. I can remember, even now, how good it was on a bright moonlit night sledging down the hill into the hedge at the bottom. Oh! the hot-aches in your fingers and the chilblains, but I thought it was well worth it.'

Margaret learned to cook from watching and helping her mother making stews and milk puddings in the small oven and trying to fry on the open fire. Lovely toast was made by holding the bread in front of the fire, then spreading it with home-made dripping. That was unless the bread was dropped in the ashes!

Christmas seemed a long time coming, but children started to get excited very early, as soon as bonfire night had gone. Margaret's mother gradually accumulated the ingredients to make mince pies, Christmas puddings and a Christmas cake. Margaret liked to watch the preparations, but neither she nor her brother were encouraged to help, being considered more of a hindrance. The only helpful thing allowed was licking their fingers when cleaning out the bowls, including her mother's big brown crock bowl. One task they were given was to pick the gritty stones from the raisins, grate both the apples and the suet, which was bought in a lump from the butcher. Eggs had to be cracked individually into a basin, not mixed together, in case there was a bad one. When she was ready the two children would watch their mother put a couple of silver threepenny bits in the mixture then they could make a wish. The pudding would have to steam for hours, filling the kitchen with vapour until the windows ran with water. Women had some horrible jobs to do, such as plucking and drawing a chicken, (that is removing the birds innards) and skinning rabbits. These tasks appeared to have been taken in their stride.

Margaret went carol singing with a group from the Sunday school. The children walked round the village carrying candles in jam jars, calling at the houses. Christmas decorations were mostly home-made, paper lanterns and paper chains were glued together with flour and water paste. Margaret does not remember having had a Christmas tree, but no doubt they were just as pleased to see a branch of a fir tree with the home-made decorations on it. Chestnuts were roasted on the bars of the fire and they tasted lovely, even the burned bits.

The same ritual was followed every Christmas day. Margaret and her brother woke early to look through the contents of their Christmas stockings, which contained annuals, crayons, magic painting books and various knitted garments. Dinner consisted of chicken, with the wishbone to be pulled, followed by plum pudding. Later there were cards and board games to play. For tea, the family had salmon sandwiches, fruit trifle with cream, probably evaporated milk, and Christmas cake. On Boxing Day the two children would visit friends and compare Christmas presents.

Margaret says, 'I do not remember seeing in the New Year, but then sitting by a crackling wireless did not appeal to me.'

This ends Margaret's memories of life in the village. She was happy there and enjoyed it. She never felt deprived because everybody lived the same way. After fifty years there was a reunion in the village hall, where she met up again with all her old school friends and remembered them all. Although Margaret's life was changed considerably by the war, she was fortunate in that she was living with her mother and brother. Mainly it was the women, who had to cope with very difficult situations. Returning to Coventry at the end of the war Margaret was of an age to begin working.

Jean Appleton

This article is taken from a taped recording first produced for blind listeners. The author wishes to remain anonymous.

Anne McInulty (nee Rainbow)

In the years before the bombing of the Second World War, Coventry retained much of its medieval pattern of narrow streets and crowded courts, which became such a feature of the city. It was in one such court that Anne McInulty was born in April 1923 at 4ct 3h Spon Street, the sixth of seven children. The entrance to the court still exists where the newsagents and butcher's shop are situated, but the yard and buildings are long gone. Typical of many courts, the houses were built around a central paved yard with no back entrances, just the front door. There was no water or electricity laid on, just gas for lighting and a range for cooking. Water was taken from a pump in the yard and a row of three toilets were shared by the six houses in the court. At the end of the yard was the slaughterhouse for the butcher's shop in Spon Street.

Anne's father worked at the Morris factory in Gosford Street, but work was often intermittent, two weeks in and two weeks out. To supplement the family's meagre income he had an allotment in Allesley Old Road, where he grew potatoes and root vegetables, runner beans and rhubarb. A pig was raised between the allotment holders and shared when it was slaughtered. Their food was plain but filling and the only food that was rationed during periods of short time was bread.

It was while they lived in Spon Street that Anne started school at St. John's in Dover Street. Like all the family she was christened at St. John's church nearby. In 1931 the family were moved to Bulwer Road on the new Hill Farm Estate, Radford, due to slum clearance of some of the old courts. Anne attended Radford School until the age of eleven when she went to Barker's Butts School.

Anne's mother was ill for many years with tuberculosis before she died in 1934. After he was widowed her father worked nights to enable him to see the children off to school or work, after he had finished his shift, before going to bed. With the help of Anne's second oldest sister, Kit, they managed the home and family, with her father paying her insurance stamp. He was a very competent cook, for he had been doing the majority of the cooking for many years before his wife died. He made wonderful Christmas puddings, steamed for hours in the copper. Being an engineer, he manufactured a system of shelves to fit inside the copper, on which were stacked enough puddings to cover Christmas Day, Boxing Day, New Year's Day and each child's birthday. He made the cleaning of the fruit and preparation a game in which they all took part.

Anne's father went to town every Monday morning, as he had not been working the night before. He would go to Glenn's sweet shop in Hales Street to buy two quarters of sweets and was given another two quarters free (so the concept of buy one get one free has been around a long time). That was to last the family a whole week. He then went for a couple of pints in The Turk's Head in Silver Street. Every time he went off on these trips he would say the same phrase. 'I'm going out and I'm going to find some woman and she's going to come back and sort you bloody lot out.'

When Anne left school at fourteen she began work at Cash's. She found the work tedious and boring; being a dog's body was not her idea of a fulfilling occupation. The wages were only 10/- per week, minus stoppages and she knew she could do better. After two years she moved on to Leigh Mills making the material for khaki uniforms, as the war had just started. To begin with she was on an automatic machine, which paid well as they were on piecework. Unfortunately the man who set up these machines joined the forces and left, leaving the company without a skilled man to set them up, so Anne like the others, had to go on to a Jacquard loom (or pick and pick machine as Anne called it). It was slower and her wages decreased in consequence. After two months she gave in her notice and left.

Anne McInulty

The Labour Exchange sent her to Alfred Herbert's factory in Edgwick. She enjoyed being at Herbert's where she worked on a capstan making machine parts. With wages of £4 per week and a bonus scheme at the end of the month she was far better off than at her previous occupations in weaving.

All the smaller machines were operated by women, who took over many of the factory jobs normally done by men, as they joined the forces and went off to war. Generally it was the skilled men, older men and boys who continued to work in the factories. There was a great camaraderie between the workers. Despite the environment Herbert's was kept very clean. Floors were spotless on Monday morning, although it became a bit dirtier as the week progressed. As Anne said the shop floor was the shop window at Herbert's, with numerous visitors being shown around. She remained there for the whole of the war and was very happy.

Anne always had trouble getting to work on time; she just could not wake up in the morning. Management tolerated her lack of punctuality because she was an excellent worker. One morning, late as usual, she was just taking her hair rollers out when she was called into the office where her foreman, Mr Eastwood, handed her a pass-out. 'What's that for?' said Anne. 'Go home and finish your sleep out and let's have you back here on time,' he replied. Irate at this instruction, she took the pass, but instead of going out she went to the office and gave in her notice. She was filling in the forms when the foreman came down and tried to persuade her not to leave. Once she had set her mind on leaving there was no going back and she went. After a short spell at the Humber factory, which she found really filthy, she did return to Alfred Herbert's for another five years after the war. Although initially she did not get her bonus at the end of the month, for Mr Eastwood was getting his own back, at the end of another month it was back to normal.

The war meant a lot of changes in the family. Anne's two brothers went into the forces and her sisters began to get married. Her sister Kit, had married her husband George, early in the war. Anne looked upon her almost as a mother, for she had taught Anne all that she knew about household management, shopping and cooking and had helped to bring up the family and supported their father. When he died in 1942, the Council transferred the tenancy of the family house to Kit and George and they remained there for the rest of their lives, eventually buying it from the council. All the sisters were married from there.

Weddings presented their own problems during the war due to shortages of food and clothing, soldiers being away and bomb damage to property. Anne was courting her husband to be, Jock, in 1940 and was asked to be bridesmaid to his sister Mary at her wedding on 16th November 1940. She had arranged to have her bridesmaid dress made by a Mrs Hackett of Norman Place Road. It was made of red velvet trimmed with silver lace, with a silver Juliet cap, and the small bridesmaid had the same. The bride, who was going to borrow a dress and veil for the occasion, liked Anne's dress so much she asked Mrs Hackett to make one in satin, trimmed with gold lace for herself. The problem of getting hold of material was not so great in 1940 as it became later in the war.

They arranged to hold the reception at the Co-op in Smithford Street and had taken the wedding cake and all their presents there on Thursday afternoon, 14th November 1940. The blitz that occurred that night destroyed the building and everything inside. The bride and groom and their families were in a quandary what to do. The family home in Radford was not affected by the bombing, but was too small to hold the reception there, even if they could provide enough food, which was doubtful. The bridegroom, Peter, cycled to Christ the King church where the service was to be held and the priest agreed to go ahead with the ceremony. Cars had been arranged to take them to the church and reception and luckily they were still able to function. They agreed to pick everyone up at a specified house and find a route to the church, for there was great disruption to traffic. Peter's mother had a larger house in Earlsdon Avenue and they all gathered there.

On the morning of the wedding there was much activity at the house in Earlsdon Avenue. It was considered bad luck for the bride and groom to see each other before their arrival at the church and Anne had to precede Mary wherever she went in the house, warning Peter to get out of the way. Eventually the cars arrived and took the bride and her attendants in one car to the church, via Coundon Station. The station and line had been damaged in the blitz and a crew of workmen were busy repairing the line. As the car drove past the workmen stood up and cheered at the happy sight of the bride and bridesmaids. It was very emotional and they all arrived at the church in tears.

Back at Earlsdon Avenue after the ceremony they drank a toast to the happy couple and had a piece of Christmas cake, used in place of the destroyed wedding cake, then they all went to Ma Cooper's pub for a drink. Anne being too young to enter a pub was dispatched to the fish and chip shop in Albany Road to buy a meal for all the guests. This was one meal that did not require coupons and despite the long queue she was served with numerous portions of fish and chips for the wedding breakfast. Unknown to Anne and probably the whole queue the King and Queen were visiting Kensington Laundry, just around the corner in Kensington Road at the time. It was certainly a wedding to remember.

On the morning after the November blitz Anne and Jock walked through Broadgate to see for themselves the devastation caused to the city centre. From there they walked to Grangemouth Road where Jock's mother lived, to see an amazing sight. Suspended between her house and the one next door was a landmine. Its parachute had snagged on the guttering and it hung dangerously above the gap. The ARP managed to cushion the sides very carefully to prevent it striking the walls of the houses and waited for the bomb disposal forces to arrive and defuse it. Jock and his family had been in the shelter that night, although Anne and her family usually stayed in the house during a raid. Anne remembers, with some humour that on that night a blast outside blew the blackout curtain down. In an instant a voice from nowhere shouted out, 'Get that bloody light out.' From that point they sought shelter with their neighbours. They took their old dog, Trixie, who was about sixteen with them. When the raid was over the poor dog had become demented, just howling continuously. As no vet was available to put an end to her misery, Anne's father drowned her in the rainwater butt.

Anne cannot remember any problem obtaining food. With rationing everyone had a fair share of provisions. Perhaps because they had never been used to luxuries they were able to cope better than some. Their ration books were lodged with the Co-op and they were guaranteed those goods. They did not spend time queuing for food, but they did have to queue for cigarettes. She began smoking when she was on nightshift at Alfred Herbert's. She worked two weeks nights and two weeks days. The shift lasted from 7pm-7.30am with two half hour breaks from 11.30pm-12midnight and 4-4.30am. Not being used to these late hours she had trouble keeping awake (she obviously needed her sleep). A woman she worked with gave her a cigarette to keep her awake and she continued from then onwards. They cost 4.1/2d for 10 Woodbines, 10d for 10 Players or Senior Service and another brand called Passing Cloud, which cost more and tasted awful, but if there was nothing else you had no choice.

Clothing coupons were not enough to fulfil all your needs, but you made do with what you had. You passed clothes on to someone else, or if you were good at needlework you altered them, if not you found someone who could. When war broke out Anne was only sixteen and had not stopped growing, which made life more difficult. Skirts were fairly short, just below knee length. Not until after the war, when the New Look came in did skirts lengthen.

For entertainment the family occasionally went to the cinema or the theatre. When the war first started such places were closed for fear of air raids, but soon opened again when the authorities realised that it was not going to happen immediately and because it was a morale booster. When they resumed, programmes were over early and cinemas closed by 9pm. Buses also ceased at 9pm, which restricted travel and was an incentive to be home early. One night Anne and Jock were at the Rialto Cinema when the siren went. Anne insisted that they should go home, as her father would be worried about her. They dodged from one shelter to another, despite the shrapnel and shouts of the wardens. They made it safely!

Anne's sister, Joan, had married in 1940 and she and her husband, Leonard, lived in Bedworth. Their child, Kathleen Anne, was born at George Eliot Hospital, but when the hospital was bombed that night, mother and daughter were sent home to Bedworth after 24 hours. There she could have the care and attention she needed. When Kathleen Anne was about a year old they moved back to Coventry to a house in Links Road, Radford. Leonard had been suffering from a pain in his side for some time, but the doctor in Bedworth was not concerned. When they registered with Dr. Rollins in Coventry, he sent him straight into Keresley Hospital, as the pain was due to appendicitis. At about the same time Joan had suffered a miscarriage and was confined to bed. Anne and Jock went to see Leonard in hospital after his operation and he was still complaining of the pain in his side.

Anne was not very sympathetic, as she had been operated on for appendicitis just before the outbreak of war and thought he was making rather a fuss. However, she felt dreadful about her reaction when Joan was sent for, as her husband was so seriously ill. She had to get out of her bed and make her way through snow to the hospital, where Leonard died of peritonitis. Anne went with Joan to register the death in Coventry, only to be told that Keresley was out of their jurisdiction and it had to be registered in Meriden. They went to view Leonard's body in the mortuary, then situated just behind the Fire Station, in Pool Meadow. It was a shock to see him pulled out on a shelf in the cold store.

This was not the only tragedy to hit Joan; her young daughter, Kathleen Anne, began suffering from epileptic fits at the age of seven months, as a result of being given the whooping cough vaccine. As soon as she was given the injection she went into a fit and continued to suffer from them all her life and died at the age of 52 during an epileptic fit. Joan remarried in 1944 to an old friend she had known before she married Leonard. They too had a daughter, born in 1945. All pregnant women had to sleep downstairs during the war, presumably because it was thought there would be more protection or for ease of access to a shelter.

Although none of Anne's brothers and sisters lost their lives in the war, the loss of their father in 1942 at the age of 54 had been a blow. Anne and Jock had become engaged in that same year. Jock was working at the Morris factory making tanks, when he and a friend volunteered for the Fleet Air Arm. Although the friend was soon in that service, Jock was put in the army instead, eventually being transferred to the Black Watch Regiment. He and Anne married in 1944 and he had the opportunity to become a regular soldier at the end of the war when he was serving in Germany. Anne was reluctant as there were no married quarters at the time and she did not want to be separated for long periods, so he did not go ahead.

After the war Anne had numerous jobs, but eventually worked in the kitchen at Ullathorne School, where she remained until she retired. Her only regret in life is that she did not have a family, for she would have loved children. Unfortunately that pleasure was denied to her, although she has a very close relationship with her nephews and nieces. Sadly Jock died in 1985 but she still lives in Styvechale where she and Jock spent many happy years together. She looks back on the war in a very pragmatic way, with a clear recall of events. They had to get through it and they did.

Lynn Hockton

Interviewed March 2006

Women in Wartime

'What did you do in the war, Mummy?' I expect many mothers have been asked that question. What did women do during the war? If you had children under school age, you were not directed into essential war work or military service. My daughter was born in 1940, so I was in that category.

At the outbreak of war in 1939, life was very different. There were few washing machines or refrigerators and no microwave ovens. Many houses had no hot water or central heating. There was no television, only 'wireless' (radio): no supermarkets and little packaging. Consequently housework and shopping took much longer. Many things had to be weighed and also we had to queue for goods in short supply. Rationing became more stringent as the war progressed.

With all the difficulties, we tried to make life as normal as possible. Clothes became rationed and 'make do and mend' was introduced, so out came our sewing machines! We made quite elegant dresses out of curtain material, which was not rationed and I remember making a skirt out of my husband's grey flannel trousers.

In spite of the blackout, cinemas and theatres remained open, but we were reluctant to leave our children because of fear of bombing. I was a member of the local Women's Institute (WI) in Allesley, Coventry, which met in the afternoon. As the village hall and school were used as Decontamination and First Aid centres, the meetings were held at private houses, which had

Dorothy Parker

large enough rooms to hold so many people. The offshoots of the WI were a Produce Guild and a Handicraft Guild, a drama group and a choir. This was directed by the church organist, the accompanist was his wife. There were few 'play groups' and these were reserved for mothers in war work, so we took the children with us. There were probably five or six children, who played happily on the rugs at the end of the room and very rarely did we have to tell them to be quiet. They knew they were expected to behave properly. From this choir, some of us founded a singing group, and as a quartet we entertained other women's groups in the area. This was much enjoyed and we had a lot of fun. We met in each other's houses and our children came with us. Many ingenious recipes were tried out at these inevitable tea parties.

Another offshoot of the WI was gardening classes, through which the members decided to buy a canning machine! By this time some of the toddlers had started school, but I was still not eligible for call-up due to age, so I was able to take full advantage of the canning machine. We made the most of any surplus fruit and vegetables from our allotments and gardens – mostly plums and tomatoes. Again we met in the house of those who had a large enough kitchen. Occasionally there was the inevitable disaster! Through inefficient sealing, the canner 'blew up' and there would be tomatoes or plums all over the kitchen. This caused great hilarity and much patience on the part of the householder. These canning sessions would take all day, and as schools had much longer dinner breaks, the children joined us for a picnic lunch. In the evening we spent hours knitting socks, scarves, gloves, etc., some for our own use and a lot for the armed forces. Despite the constant threat of an air raid we carried on knitting.

Public transport was limited and petrol was rationed, so we walked or took our bikes. With a child's seat on the crossbar we would cycle into the country to pick blackberries, which we bottled. All of this took time, which added to the strain of a woman's day. There was always the threat of an air raid, which meant that we always carried our gas masks. In spite of all this we would pool our resources and have picnics in the local fields or parks. Life went on. Although the war in Europe was over in 1945, shortages became worse and rationing continued into the early 1950s.

There was a Barrage Balloon site in fields off Kingsbury Road, opposite the bottom of Forfield Road where we lived, which was manned by the Women's Auxiliary Air Force (WAAF). After the war temporary housing was built on the site to house displaced persons, and eventually Sherbourne Fields School. We were asked by the government to allow these WAAF girls to have a bath at our house. They were allowed two baths a week, for which we were paid the sum of one shilling per bath. Needless to say, these 'bath nights' became very popular. In fact, I kept in touch with one of the WAAF girls until she died last year (2006).

What did women do during the war?
I think we kept on keeping on.

Dorothy Parker

65

The Women's Voluntary Service

The Women's Voluntary Service (WVS) was established in 1938 by Stella Issacs, Dowager Marchioness of Reading and widow of Rufus Issacs, who was Governor of India from 1921-25. In the early 1930s she had been very active with the Personal Service League; this was a charity providing clothes for the unemployed.

At a meeting held at the Home Office, in May 1938, it was agreed that a new organisation be formed with Lady Reading in charge. She chose women that she knew and trusted and of course, they were from a specific social class. The Vice-chairman was Priscilla Norman, who was the wife of the governor of the Bank of England. The Chief Administrator was Mrs. Lyndsay Huxley, who was the Honorary Treasurer of the National Federation of Women's Institutes.

The WVS was a voluntary organisation. At local level no one held a specific rank, they could be a group leader one week and the next week be part of the team.

I was surprised to learn that the women had to buy their own uniforms, although I believe they did get extra clothing coupons. Of course not all of the women had uniforms, but wore the WVS badge on their everyday clothes. The uniform comprised a green felt hat with a maroon band, a grey/green tweed overcoat and a grey/green tweed skirt. They also wore a maroon blouse, in artificial silk or wool, and a striped woollen scarf in these colours. Brown brogue shoes completed the outfit. The uniforms were often referred to as 'old spinach and rhubarb'.

At the outbreak of war the WVS had 165,000 volunteer members, involved in various tasks, and their work covered a very wide spectrum. By 1941 there were one million women in the organisation. They organised first-aid courses in the cities that they thought would be the targets of the Luftwaffe. They put these in place, but did not provide training as this had to be done by qualified staff.

In 1939 Lady Reading broadcast to America appealing for clothing. Known as 'Bundles for Britain' donated items were sent, by the American Red Cross, and distributed by the WVS Emergency Clothing Stores.

These unpaid women gave up their leisure, comfort and sleep, to minister to the needs of anyone who called upon them for their services. They darned socks for servicemen and cleaned military hospitals. Meals were cooked for air raid victims on emergency stoves made from bricks gathered from the bombed buildings and also helped at control centres. The volunteers also provided canteen facilities for the Home Guard and for wounded soldiers at railway stations. Members also sat up with invalids and expectant mothers, during the blitz, and recovered the belongings of those made homeless by bombing.

The organisation was very active in Coventry. Mrs Helen Brooke took charge in the early days and members initially, did great work, firstly in recruiting women and then helping to provide material comforts for the services. She retired due to health reasons and Councillor Mrs Hyde took over the organisation.

Pearl Hyde did wonderful work as the leader of the Coventry WVS; she was large, blonde and the daughter of a publican. When she first came to Coventry, she fell under the influence of Emily Smith, who was a pioneer of the local Labour movement, she brought Pearl into the Labour Party and ultimately she won a seat on the City Council. She was definitely a woman of the people. As a leader she showed that she could exercise authority, but she would never ask anyone to do anything she was not prepared to do herself. Later in 1957/8 she became a very successful Lord Mayor of Coventry.

The WVS was also responsible for the evacuation of people. Mrs Elsie Beaufoy was responsible for organising rest centres in Shirley and at times was required, at two hours notice, to provide beds and food for a large number of people.

When Gulson Hospital, Coventry was bombed WVS members were soon on the scene providing soup and refreshments for the staff and patients. There were mobile canteens on Pool Meadow, Coventry and a person recalled Pearl Hyde distributing food to the people who had been bombed out of their homes. The WVS was called to Hill Street Gasworks, Coventry, where they must have encountered a horrific scene, as there were dead bodies all over the street. When the Despatch Riders were asked if they had eaten, they said their last meal had been the previous day. Immediately the women started to serve mugs of tea and sandwiches. This must have been awful in these macabre surroundings.

The WVS was also responsible for salvage drives. People sent in saucepans and kettles to be melted down as they contained Bauxite and this was needed for aircraft production. They were also involved in the collection of paper salvage, milk bottle tops and old books for pulping. There were ranges of grants given to people in need. Homeless people could apply for clothing vouchers to get emergency clothes from the Drapers Hall. When Coventry and Warwickshire Hospital, Stoney Stanton Road, Coventry was bombed the WVS arrived and provided hot soup; a nurse said it was like manna from heaven. They cared for those devastated by the bombing such as tired, homeless, women and children wandering amongst the ruins of the bombed buildings. In the wintry cold, their vans took hot meals to those people in need. It was said that the WVS was an inspiration to everyone.

Survivors taking refreshments from a mobile canteen manned by the Women's Voluntary service

The WVS also ran the National Savings Campaign; this was to encourage savings to fund the war effort. As a small child I can remember being dragged around the streets in the district by my mother and calling at many houses. People had a card on which to stick the stamps they had purchased; these stamps were to the value of six pence or two shillings and sixpence. I do not know if my mother was a member of the WVS. I hated having to go with her as she used to have a little chat with the householders. In those days children were not allowed to listen to grown up conversations, so I used to be bored and could not wait for my mother to finish.

Researching old copies of the *Coventry Standard* and *Midland Daily Telegraph*, I came across many interesting items of news. Some members gave up their Christmas Day to cook a special meal for the troops. Servicemen who called at the headquarters, which at this time was in Priory Row, were always assured of getting a cup of tea. They sent toys, sweets and clothes to evacuated children and to hospital patients. They even provided a bed for a refugee who was without a home.

In the *Coventry Standard* dated 6th January 1940, there were many letters of thanks. Councillor Pearl Hyde sent her thanks to all the Coventry WVS women for the work that they had done during the past year.

Members had knitted socks for Finnish soldiers as they were considered a dire necessity. A letter was received from a Finnish lady, Ingrid Peirson, thanking the WVS for the large bundle of socks that she had received for her countrymen, who were fighting in the Arctic regions. The socks had been sent by special aeroplane and had arrived just before Christmas. Pearl Hyde said that she was continuing with her efforts to send further warm things to Finland and appealed for more help.

A letter was also received from Helen Corcoran, who was the teacher-in-charge of Southam R.C School and also from the Sacred Heart School in Coventry. They thanked the WVS for the clothing and woollies which were much appreciated by the evacuees. Mrs. C.M. Matthews of Dunchurch, Rugby, wrote thanking them for sending blankets and clothes. She had been able to fit out several very needy children and stated that most of the evacuees were boys.

An evacuee child at Burton Dassett, who was living just outside the village of Northend, wrote and said that her teacher, Miss Lee, had told the girls that a parcel had been received from the WVS. This child received a knitted vest, pixie hood and a scarf and she was thrilled with them. A letter was written by a soldier thanking the volunteers for the help they had given him and that he had now reached his camp after a long day of travelling. An airman wrote thanking the WVS for the parcel that they had sent him. He said that he was working continuously, at sea and on the coast, and this kind gesture was appreciated, particularly during the cold weather. The Chief Billeting Officer for Meriden Rural District Council sent his thanks for the parcels of clothing and toys that he had received and said that these had been distributed to their three parishes. There was also a letter from the Balsall Common Billeting Officer asking if it would be possible to get a suit for a boy aged fourteen.

A letter was received from W.W. Ward, who was the Public Assistance Officer, thanking the WVS for games and toys that had been sent to Town Thorns and to nursery children at Cheltenham. The Rev. Paul Stacy also wrote thanking them for getting toys and sweets and for distributing them. He quoted 'Mere men would make a slow job of it'. This is very true Eight pounds of Brazil Chocolate was sent for the inmates of Exhall Institution. The Matron of another city hospital wrote thanking them for sweets and toys for the children at Christmas. The Head Teacher of St. Michael's School, Polesworth, wrote a letter of thanks for the chocolates and said that they would be distributed at the children's Christmas Party. The Head also said that she was able to use the clothes that had also been received for three large children who had just arrived at the school. The Head Teacher of St.

Michael's and All Saints School in Coventry said that the Christmas Party had been a success, and she was very much indebted to Coventry WVS for arranging the entertainment.

In the *Midland Daily Telegraph* dated 29th May 1940, the Coventry service appealed for more recruits, even if women could spare some part of a day or week. The demands of the WVS were growing both in volume and scope. At the moment they were involved in a big task distributing ration books, canvassing for billets and for the provision of new brick and concrete Air Raid Precautions (ARP) shelters and also doing sick bay duties. The article went on to point out that these women were not paid, despite the impression held by many citizens. Whilst receiving an ever-increasing demand, for their assistance, they were losing many members who were leaving to go to work in the factories in response to the appeal for women. Urgent needs included women to act as nurses in mobile units, also as ambulance drivers and for all kinds of work. Any women who felt that they could help were asked to get in touch with the WVS Headquarters at 11 Priory Row, Coventry.

On the 13th July 1940 the *Coventry Standard*, under the heading *'Work in Wartime'* included a report by Pearl Hyde in which she made reference to the feeding of the troops. She said that the mobile canteen, sited at the station, had proved to be a real boon. It had been presented to the WVS by Mr. H.H. Harley of Coventry Gauge and Tool Limited. In three months 10,000 portions of light refreshments had been handed out by the women staffing it. This was valuable as it was used by servicemen who were passing through Coventry and also men arriving on the late trains. Refreshments were often supplemented with cakes or pies cooked by the WVS members themselves. The canteen was also available to serve civil defence workers anywhere in the city if any air raid damage was caused. Thanks from the men had more than repaid the women for the work they had done. Gifts such as milk, cigarettes, tea, biscuits and other items had been received from various people; these were the means which enabled canteens to function. Canteen workers were also supplied to military establishments and the WVS had arranged refreshments for factory workers.

Mrs Hyde went on to talk about brick shelters and said that a survey of the city had taken place. Fifteen thousand applications had been received for them, the paperwork delivered to the WVS office and a proportion completed. It was hard work for the canvassers having so many homes to visit and sometimes having to go back a number of times. Several of the members worked daily at the Development Office, preparing work for the Engineers' Department. The results returned by the canvassers were remarkable and valuable data had been compiled. Mrs Hyde stated 'the work was done cheerfully and well'.

Mrs Hyde also said that at the request of the Ministry of Labour the WVS had commenced a street canvass, looking for prospective billets, and work was still proceeding. Up to date 1,850 billets had been procured. Each householder had been approached and the information obtained was invaluable. Details required were the type of accommodation, the terms, when available, sex of lodger and number of rooms. Each day a billeting officer reported to the council's Chief Billeting Officer and gave particulars concerning the progress. Emergency billets had been procured for families and factory workers from evacuated areas.

With regard to rationing, daily rotas of 100 voluntary workers were supplied to the Food Office and the workers devoted all of their time to any tasks required. The Food Officer Mr L Fox paid tribute to the excellent voluntary help he had received.

Clerical staff had been sent to the ARP office and several S.O.S calls had been received from that department, during the previous month, and had been promptly dealt with. Another direction in which help had been given was in distributing clothing to evacuees. The Public Assistance Committee had approved of the WVS office being the central depot from which officers of refugees should apply after an air raid, for clothing and other items. Parcels of men's, women's and children's clothing of all sizes had been distributed to all relief stations. Applications had also been received from the City Aid Soldiers and Sailors Help Society and similar bodies for help in deserving cases. More help had been given to speeding up recruiting for the Civil Nursing Reserve and thousands of casualty bags had been made for the Public Health Department. Publicity had been given to the WVS in propaganda for the National Savings Campaign.

Finally, Mrs Hyde said that all who were in touch with the work of the WVS in Coventry would agree that it was doing valuable work and taking an active part towards winning the war.

A full account of the huge task, undertaken by the WVS, regarding billets was given in the *Midland Daily Telegraph* dated 31st July 1940. It stated that they organised a system of canvassing for billets for industrial workers coming to work in Coventry. Their task began by calling on 29,000 households in the city with the questionnaire. It was such a major task for the volunteers that it was decided, with a view to easing the transport problem, that the city be divided into areas for which members would be personally responsible. Each of the canvassers would be furnished with a certificate accompanying the book into which entries, in answer to the questions, would be made. The survey was to be completed in the shortest possible time, as there were many households to visit. It was pointed out that householders should be encouraged to offer any spare accommodation, as in the majority of cases Coventry was attracting workers of a very good type. It was also reported that some canvassers had complained about the bad treatment they had received, from certain householders, whilst doing their survey. A number were most discourteous. Mr James Taylor, the Chief Billeting Officer of Coventry, said 'it would be appreciated if householders would notify the billeting headquarters at 10a Hay Lane, Coventry of any accommodation they had to offer. The billets needed to be within reasonably close proximity to the factories'.

On the 9th September 1940 women were called upon to assist in many directions in the event of the city being targeted by enemy raiders, this was to be in the form of the Housewives Service. No training would be necessary for women who offered to help and five or six women would be required in each street. They needed to put a WVS card marked Housewives Service, in their house window, so if the city was raided or damaged, they were required to help in any way they were able. To help the air-raid wardens, they had to deposit buckets of water and sand on their doorsteps at night and had to be prepared to give temporary assistance to the injured and homeless people until appropriate services arrived. If wardens, police or Auxiliary Fire Service men were engaged for any length of time, the housewives would boil water for tea or provide accommodation for temporary rest. Women who offered help had to enrol at the WVS headquarters in Priory Row, Coventry.

The WVS did a local collection of kitchen waste for pig feeding. They appealed to householders for containers to enable the collection to be carried out. They particularly needed empty oil drums, old fashioned tin baths or barrels, which had to hold approximately five gallons or more and preferably with a lid and to be easy to clean. For householders who could help, but could not take the containers to the WVS offices, arrangements were made for these to be collected by the Corporation Parks Department.

Early in December 1940 it was reported that the WVS headquarters had been destroyed in the air raid on 14th November 1940. All their books and records were lost, so they moved to Drapers Hall, Bayley Lane, Coventry. Members were asked to report to the new headquarters, so that fresh records of their members could be compiled. Due to enemy activity the WVS had their stores of woollen items damaged by fire. The knitted articles were for the services and the members were asked to return finished garments to the Drapers Hall as soon as possible.

On the 16th December 1940 an appeal was made in Coventry for thirty full-time women ambulance drivers and also for an additional number to volunteer for part-time service.

It was reported in the *Midland Daily Telegraph* on the 23rd December 1940 that the Coventry WVS were making a tour of the city's public shelters during the hours of darkness, on Christmas Eve, to distribute toys to all the children. Mrs Hyde said that they had a wonderful assortment of toys. She sent Christmas Greetings to all her volunteers and grateful thanks to all the citizens, who had supported their work throughout the year. The public air raid shelters had no chimneys, so Santa Claus in the cheerful guise of members of the WVS, went down the steps, carrying bulky parcels for the children. A fleet of cars, some belonging to helpers and some loaned by the police, took part in the distribution of toys and clothes that had been sent to Coventry by sympathisers from all over the country. Firstly, they went to a large public shelter in Spon Street, Coventry and visited other bigger shelters in the poorer districts of the city. They arrived at Spon Street, shortly after dark, to find various compartments in the shelter decorated with paper streamers and evergreens by people who were determined to have a happy Christmas, bombers or no bombers. The children whooped with joy as they gathered round the parcel-laden women. Where the need was more obvious, new clothing instead of toys were given to the children. The distributions went on well into the night.

When Coventry Cathedral was bombed, it lost almost all of its possessions. In 1953 a new processional cross was presented by the Dowager Marchioness of Reading, in memory of the war service of the WVS. It was dedicated at a service on the 14th May 1953, Ascension Day. The service was attended by 500 members and was given in memory of those who had fallen.

When the present Queen ascended the throne, she became patron of the WVS and in 1966 they had the honour of adding Royal to the title, becoming the WRVS.

At Coventry and Warwickshire Hospital, Stoney Stanton Road, the café, which is used by the outpatients, is manned by the WRVS and in some places they deliver meals on wheels to the elderly and also run lunch clubs.

It is difficult to overstate the importance of the work that the WVS did during the blitz. People who had lost their homes and possibly members of their family had someone that they could turn to. Although the rest centres may not have been like hotels at least they provided a roof and food.

We must remember that these volunteers were just ordinary women doing a wonderful job and obviously seeing some horrific sights.

Lady Reading said 'We know we look shabby and we know our members are not young, but we are proud of the fact that we are trusted by the ordinary people'. How very true.

Angela Atkin

Acknowledgements
Thank you to Coventry Central Library – Local Studies for their help.
Within The Island Fortress (WVS) Jon Mills.
Thanks also to Vic Terry for his assistance.

Bibliography
Newspaper Cuttings from the *Midland Daily Telegraph* 1940
and the *Coventry Standard* 1940

Photograph of WVS Mobile Canteen
Taken from *The Bombing of Coventry* 1940. Compiled by David Rimmer, City Archivist.

Betty Saltiel

Betty Saltiel was a resident of Coventry for nearly forty years. She taught in many junior schools in the city until her retirement. She wrote this piece about her experiences as an evacuee for a project being carried out by a local school in 2001. She went to talk to the children about those experiences to illustrate what it was like to live in times of war. She was a member of the Women's Research Group for two and a half years and contributed articles to this and the last book. Sadly Betty died in October 2006, but will be remembered by all those who met her through the many interests in which she was involved.

I was evacuated twice: the first time to Norfolk on 30th August 1939 just four days before war was declared and I was ten years old. The first eight or nine months of the war little seemed to be happening for those on the 'home front' and by the summer of 1940 my brother Bernard, cousin Marie and I were brought home to London. That summer air raids began and my mother took my brother Bernard and me away again, this time to Northamptonshire. The difference between the first and the second time was that in 1939 I went with my own school and all the girls I had known from the age of five, but the children I accompanied on the second evacuation were completely unknown to me. What I did not realise at the time, was that, but for a few rare and brief occasions, I would never again see girls I went through junior school with, except for one of my best friends who lived nearby.

I well remember the day I was evacuated the first time. Since my mother was a helper and coming with us, the only one left at home in London was my dad. He would miss us, but all his family and my mother's family lived very near to us so he would not feel too isolated. We had been waiting for what seemed like hours for the train at the little station opposite our school. We sat with coats on, our little bags of clean clothes and gas masks in cardboard boxes slung across our shoulders. When the time came for us to move off we found the street filled with crowds of people, mostly parents, waiting to see us off. As we crossed the road I could see the bald head of a short man straining to see - us! My dad had left home very early that morning as usual (as a London taxi driver he worked long hours), but at some point he had decided to park the cab he was driving and wait to see us into the station. The long wait and the uncertainty of the day - for none of us knew where we were going - and then my dad's appearance brought home to me that my family was being split up and I burst into tears. My teacher, not realising the reason for my tears, told me off, since I would have my mother with me, so what reason did I have for crying, and that did not help at all.

To keep siblings together, the young ones went with the older children, so my brother, who was a six-year old infant came with me and my class. Some of my classmates had younger siblings with them, so that by the time we arrived at our destination we had quite a spread of ages. My eight-year old cousin, Marie, had gone with her thirteen-year old sister to a different destination, but as soon as her sister turned fourteen she returned to London to go to work and Marie was left alone. Largely through my mother's efforts, Marie was brought to us in the village of Walpole St. Andrew in Norfolk and into the billet I was in. Marie and I had always been good friends and because she was younger than me, I was quite protective of her, but living together like this drew us even closer.

Marie and I lived in the centre of the very small village with an elderly couple called Mr and Mrs Eyre. They owned a few houses and some land and, we believe, were quite well-off. They had never had any children and they looked after us very well. They were kind in a way, although we were given chores to do, which were often a cause of friction. I asked my mum to find me somewhere else to live, thinking Marie would come with me, but she chose to stay with the Eyre's. I continued to visit the Eyre's largely because Marie was still there. Two particular things I do remember about Mrs Eyre; because I was an avid reader and she possessed Charlotte Bronte's *Jane Eyre* (I do not know whether she had ever read it), she gave it to me to read and it has remained a loved story ever since. I had never tasted Yorkshire pudding until I lived with the Eyre's and knew that I was experiencing something special. In the years since, I have never tasted what I now realise was the perfect Yorkshire pudding created by Mrs Eyre.

My father had not been too well and returning to London to be with him, my mother decided to stay there, but not before she had found me somewhere else to live, something she did for all the evacuees in Walpole St. Andrew. She travelled round on an rusty old bike, to ensure that both evacuees and their hosts were happy with the situation. She would then report back to the few teachers who were with us. The bike was left with me, so now that I was further from where we were being educated than I had been, I could cycle to school.

The new billet was on Black Barn Farm with Florence and Ernest Green. They were about my parents age, but had no children. There had been a baby, either stillborn or it had died soon after birth and Auntie Green never became pregnant again. She was like a mother to me. She bought me a comic every week, which she brought up to me on Sunday mornings to read in bed. She bought bright ribbon for my hair (even though I was not the ribbon type). She even cut up white ribbon from her wedding dress for me to wear. Florence had a trained contralto voice and when we washed up together, we would sing and the song I remember most was, 'When Grandpapa asked Grandmama for the second minuet.' It was wonderful living on this farm with its animals, chickens and geese.

The long path from the road to the house was flanked on either side by the fields belonging to it, in which they let the grass grow for hay during the summer of 1940. Here I played hide-and-seek in the long grass with friends. I collected the eggs every morning before I went to school and was often followed by the dog (I think his name was Prince). He would scratch at the door of our 'classroom' until realising that no one would let him in, he would go back home. I put classroom in inverted commas because it was the parish hall of the local church and a smaller room contained the infant children. We had a small field with swings, for our playground. The parish hall was large, with a dusty wooden floor and what I would describe as a furnace in the middle of the room, which kept us very warm in winter.

I sat for my 'scholarship' that year in the village school and by the time the results came I was the only one left in Walpole who had taken it there. My teacher sent me round to where the other children were being taught, with a congratulatory telegram from my family. Someone found a box of chocolates, which I took back to my own class and shared with my classmates. Things were quiet in London, so Marie, Bernard and I came home. It all happened so suddenly that I believe it upset Florence Green and although I wrote, everything between us changed.

Autumn came, there were a series of air raids and children were being packed off again to the country. We found ourselves in what I now know to be the Midlands, in a hamlet called Winwick, where seven of us were taken in by the family who lived in the Manor House, though that is not where we stayed. We were put in a flat above their large garage and meals were sent up to us on trays. As soon as we arrived I sent my parents a letter to let them know where we were. No arrangements were made to deal with our dirty clothes, so I found myself as the eldest of the seven, washing out socks and pants for the others. There was my brother Bernard and me, three sisters, one a little younger than me and two little ones, and two brothers who were about seven and eight years old. I bathed the younger ones at night. Half way through the week my mother turned up. Once she had received my letter, she got on a train with a friend of hers and the nearest place she could get to was Long Buckby. The billeting officer found them a place to stay with an elderly couple called Coles, and it was their son Frank, who brought my mother to Winwick. She did not like the situation we were in and told me to pack our bags by Saturday and she would find us somewhere to live in Long Buckby. We were in Winwick just one week, and though I denied to the sister of the 'lady' of the Manor that my mother was coming to get us, when Saturday came we were off. Again my brother and I were separated though we were just a few doors away from each other. I lived with Frank and Hilda Coles.

Long Buckby was a good place to live. It was either a very small town or a large village. It had a high street where there were shops and on the corner was the Co-op, where I loved to watch them patting the butter into oblongs to be wrapped up for customers. Next door to this was a tall door which led up to a cinema, where I saw some of the most memorable films of that time. From an early age I had often gone to the cinema in London and was really addicted. This cinema belonged to the Co-op and one got the 'divi' on the tickets bought.

I was now due to go to grammar school and had to travel into Northampton to a Catholic school called Notre Dame. My background is Jewish (unorthodox) and before I was evacuated for the second time, and because I would be with children I did not know, my mother told me not to tell anyone I was Jewish. Not long before she died, even though I really knew why, I asked her why she wanted me to keep our religion a secret. 'Because I was frightened for you,' was her reply. I had been born and brought up in a very Jewish environment: 90per cent of the girls in my school were Jewish. My mother felt we were going into strange territory and I can understand her fear.

Once again Marie was brought from somewhere to be with us, but she was not billeted with me. Once my mother was back in London for good, we three, Bernard, Marie and me made a pact to see each other every day. But some disastrous things were happening to Bernard before my mother went home and it was a while before we realised what was going on. He was a handsome little boy, with a mass of black curly hair, large brown eyes and rosy cheeks in a round, brown face. Bright and mischievous, he could be a trial at times. He was living with a couple who had a small baby, and after a while this lovely brown skin became sallow and his rosy cheeks paled, his little shoulders were hunched and the curly hair was cut so short and so badly, the curls disappeared. He was also walking badly as though his feet hurt. I do not know when we became aware of this, but probably through my mother's questions, what was happening to him became shockingly clear.

On one occasion at school Bernard asked to go to the toilet. The teacher refused, and unable to contain himself any longer, he wet himself. When he arrived home and the people he lived with discovered his wet pants he was beaten by the man of the family. This may have made him wet the bed, but from then on every night when the couple were ready for bed they would look to see if Bernard's bed was wet, and if it was he would be taken from his bed and beaten with a strap. My mother also discovered that his feet, which had been full of chilblains, had been neglected and become septic. Fortunately for us there was a woman from London, but originally from Italy, who had come to live in Long Buckby with her daughter. She rented a house and took in children who were experiencing difficulties, unhappiness, were being bullied, etc. Nurse Bordi loved those children and gave them freedom in this big rambling house. Within a few weeks Bernard's feet healed, his hair was allowed to grow and was curly once more, his cheeks grew rosy and the mischief started again. He smiled and laughed all the time. Marie and I loved visiting him there, it was such a happy household.

We were beginning to feel a yearning to be back home: things were quiet in London. One summer evening Marie and I walked down Station Road to the crossroads, talking about news reports of children who had run away to get home. We considered this and when we reached the crossroads I realised we had no money with us. 'I have 3s.2d.' said Marie. I said I would wait if she ran back to her billet and got the money. By the time she got back I realised we could not go without Bernard. To this day Marie has never let me forget this! The following evening we got Bernard and walked again to the crossroads, but we found some excuse for not going. Everyone would worry, both here and in London. We continued to do this for some evenings after that and always found reasons for not going.

I will never know why we were not brought home together. I think Marie went first, then Bernard and finally it was my turn. There must have been a reason and I never thought to ask. I have no memory of who came for me. Possibly both my parents, my dad having driven his taxi to Long Buckby. Although I was excited to see all my relatives again, grandparents, aunts, uncles and cousins and to be back in my own bedroom, I had mixed feelings. To some degree I had put down roots. Long Buckby had been home to me for nearly a year, I knew it well and had made friends. I had become attached to people I had known. This had been a learning experience of many facets, which I did not fully realise at the time. Brought up in the Jewish environment I have mentioned, I had been with people who were very different from those I had been used to. They had given me care and attention and a place to live, which became a second home. In the way that

79

many people view Jews as being odd and different, so I had felt the same about all those who were not Jewish. But the experience of living with these 'strangers' had been a revelation.

We all kept in touch with the Coles family and when Hilda died I was reunited with her daughters. I have a few regrets: the Greens in Walpole never knew how much I loved them; that I did not continue piano lessons, which had begun at school in Northampton; that I never saw so many of my primary school friends again.

What of memories: singing with Auntie Green; her pride when my scholarship results came; the mocha cake she made. Frank Coles who had to stop work as an architect when the war began and bought a little land and raised a few sheep, who let me hold his precious pens and help him when he went up to his office to do a bit of work; Hilda finger-waving my hair when it was washed; going to the fish and chip shop in the evenings on my own, for us all to have an extra supper; haymaking in one of Frank's fields and being lifted onto the cart and taken round the field at the end of a summer's day. All these things have stayed with me and would not be part of my history had it not been for the war and evacuation. Evacuation was necessary for the protection of children.

Not long after returning to London the Blitz started, but we never went away from home again.

Betty Saltiel

First compiled in July 2001 and slightly edited for this article.

Rita Smith (nee Rattigan)

When Rita was born in 1929, the youngest of five children, the family were living in Richmond Street, off Clay Lane in Coventry. As it was only a two-bedroomed house, conditions were very cramped. When Rita was four the council moved them to a three-bedroomed house in Shortley Road, Whitley. It was dark when they moved in and Rita's dad went out to explore the garden, coming back excitedly to report that the garden was enormous. In the light of the following morning, it was discovered that no dividing fences had been put up yet. What he thought was their plot, was in fact, belonging to the whole row of houses. Even so, it was a long garden and much bigger than that of their previous property.

Some six months before war broke out in 1939, Rita's father, who worked for the city council on road and building repairs, was convinced that war was coming and he was going to build an air-raid shelter in the garden. At the time he was working on reinforcing cellars in Cope Street and Cox Street with steel girders and posts. He had a gang of six strong men working under his direction and he brought them home to help him build the shelter in his garden. Constructed with the same posts and girders, with a corrugated iron roof covered with soil, it was very strong and able to withstand anything other than a direct hit. It was large enough to accommodate nineteen people, with a double bed and benches. Some of his colleagues and neighbours thought he was over-reacting to the possibility of war, but in fact he was very far-sighted.

When Rita's oldest brother, Jack, wanted to join the Territorial Army, his mother was very worried about him being called up if war began. His father made light of it, saying there was no prospect of this happening, but his actions over the shelter belied his words. He was probably trying to lessen his wife's anxiety about their son. Jack did join the Territorial Army and was called up three days before war was declared. However, he was not classed A1 as his eyesight was not perfect and his hearing was defective in one ear. He was, therefore, never on the front line of the fighting. Rita's father had served with the Medical Corps in the First World War and reached the rank of sergeant. By the Second World War he was middle aged and in a reserved occupation, as his skills at reconstruction would be in great demand.

When war was declared Rita's mother cried, worried about her children and remembering the previous war, she was well aware of the danger. Rita was nine at the time and Jack was seventeen, with Sheila, Eunice and Maurice between them. The initial fear wore off when nothing seemed to happen and they just got on with life as normal. The younger children admired Jack's uniform, although at first it consisted of many items from the First World War like puttees. When he came home on leave from the training camp the whole family went to meet the coach at Pool Meadow. Blackout material had to be purchased and made up to cover all the windows. Their ration books were lodged with the Co-op throughout the war. They were issued with gas masks, which had to be taken with them wherever they went. Life settled down into a normal rhythm again.

Rita had started at Cheylesmore School in Mile Lane soon after the family moved to Whitley. It was a long walk for a young child, following the wall of London Road Cemetery and through to Mile Lane in the company of her older siblings. They did this four times a day, for like most of their contemporaries they returned home for their midday meal and resumed lessons in the afternoon. The situation at school became chaotic once war was declared, as the authorities could not decide whether to evacuate the school or not.

The first bombs that Rita remembers were dropped on Charterhouse Road, not far from their home. It was quite a novelty and local people went to have a look at the damage caused. They all became used to bombing as raids became more frequent in the autumn of 1940, using their own shelter or public ones. One of the places where they took shelter was in Folly Lane tunnels under the railway lines. It was rather damp and uncomfortable there as there was nowhere to sit. One of Rita's sisters was very fond of hats and always insisted on bringing a hatbox, filled with her favourite hats, to the shelter with her.

On the night of 14th November 1940, her mother was airing blankets around the fire, saying she was going to spend the night in her own bed for a change, when the bombing began. The family and their neighbours retreated to the shelter in the garden in great haste. The noise was terrific and Rita sat with her fingers in her ears all night. Her father's shelter proved very effective, for when they emerged in the morning they found a scene of devastation. Immediately outside the front door was a crater, where a bomb had exploded. The doors and windows had gone and there was a hole in the roof where a manhole cover had come through and embedded itself in the floor of her brother's bedroom. The clock had stopped at 6.30am when the last bomb dropped. The blankets her mother had been airing the night before were still draped in front of the fire covered in dust and plaster. The following day, Saturday, Rita and her mother walked into the centre of Coventry to see the effects of the bombing and heard cheering when they arrived at the burnt-out shell of the cathedral. They were amazed to see the King and Queen viewing the scene. The Royal couple walked past Rita and her mother, close enough to have touched them.

The damage to their home was so great it was uninhabitable. It was decided that they would have to move out until it could be repaired and Mrs Rattigan and the three younger children went to stay with the children's grandparents in Gloucester, leaving Mr Rattigan to stay with his brother in Hen Lane. His skill was needed for the major repair work in the city. Rita's oldest sister, Sheila, was working at Armstrong Whitworth Aircraft (AWA) at Baginton by then and did not accompany the rest of the family. It is believed that she stayed with a friend. Rita had two rabbits called Blackout and Snowball that survived the bombing and she made her dad promise to look after them while she was away.

The journey to Gloucester took twelve hours, due to the disruption caused by the railway lines being blown up. There were a great many soldiers being moved to different parts of the country and they shared their carriage with them. They covered the windows with their greatcoats to stop the glass shattering over the passengers if the train was caught in a raid. They had to get out of the train at Stechford and walk through to New Street Station because the line was damaged. They had the extra burden of the cat, in the only suitable container they could find, a cardboard box with slits in the sides. He objected strongly and spent most of the journey trying to escape his confinement. However, they never brought him home again, as he had settled down and they thought another journey would be too traumatic. Once they had settled in, Rita and her brother Maurice eventually went to the local school. They had missed so much schooling that they were far behind the rest of the class. Rita would come home and cry to her granddad that she could not keep up with the rest and he tried to help her by telling her not to worry. Her sister, Eunice, who had accompanied them to Gloucester found herself a job at Brockworth nearby. They stayed there for five months before returning to Coventry just before the April 1941 blitz, although the house was not fully repaired, as it still had no glass in the windows, only a plastic-type material.

One thing that was different, the rabbits were no longer there. Rita had enquired about their health and welfare all the while that they were in Gloucester and her father always assured her that they were fine. She was surprised that they were not there, but was still given assurances that they were all right and being cared for by someone else. It was not until many years later when Rita was musing to her mother, wondering what had become of her pets. Her mother told her that her dad and his brother, Jim, had eaten them soon after she left for Gloucester. No doubt they were glad of the food in the days after the November blitz, when food was hard to come by, and he was a very good cook.

Rita and Maurice resumed their education at Earlsdon School, because Cheylesmore School had been badly damaged by incendiary bombs in November. This was quite a journey from their home in Shortley Road, too far for them to go home at midday. They took sandwiches for their lunch, Rita carrying hers in a leather knitting bag that her sister Sheila had bought for her birthday. It was purchased from Owen Owen's department store the day before the November blitz, when the building was completely burnt out. Eventually the children returned to Cheylesmore School to classes held in temporary buildings set up in the playground.

Rita had a marked artistic talent and was sent to art school in Priory Row near Hill Top. She and another pupil attended every Friday for two years. Her teacher at Cheylesmore was very interested in art and encouraged those who were artistic to draw and paint all day, rather than making them concentrate on more academic subjects. Rita entered a competition sponsored by the city council, connected with the 'Dig For Victory' campaign. The competitors had to make a poster for the campaign and when the judging took place, in a marquee set up in the War Memorial Park, Rita was placed second. They said she would have won but for the fact that she had traced the map of Britain onto her paper. It was designed with a large V over the map of Britain surrounded by vegetables. She received a letter from the Mayor congratulating her on her achievement. She loved art so much she would have liked to make it her career, but in wartime the opportunities were not available.

Not only was she good at art she was expert at knitting and sewing, a valuable skill when clothes were hard to obtain. She remembers knitting from an early age, sitting on the back doorstep at Shortley Road, clicking away with her pins making dolls' clothes. She always took her knitting into the shelter to keep busy while waiting for a raid to end. While still at school she made gloves from leftover wool with Fair Isle backs, which her two sisters sold at the factories where they worked. They were in great demand, for such items were hard to come by in the shops, even if you had the coupons. They sold for two shillings and sixpence a pair, which kept her very busy and earned her some money. Her dressmaking skills were much in demand too, altering clothes or adapting them into new styles. Her sisters were good needlewomen too, but always needed a pattern to follow, whereas Rita made up her own patterns.

Despite the bombing and disruption the family made the best of what they had. They all worked very hard and helped each other. Their father could turn his hand to anything in the building line, he grew vegetables in the garden and mended their shoes. Their mother kept the home and family together by her endeavours. Washing took the whole of Monday, with the copper to boil the clothes, baths of water for rinsing and the mangle to squeeze them as dry as possible between each process, before hanging them out to dry. Rita would help with the mangling when she came home from school and then with the ironing when it was dry. The final job for her mother was to wash the quarry-tiled floor at the end of the day. She was a good cook and managed very well with what was available. She was renowned for her puddings, but often said she was too full to eat any herself. Rita only realised in later years that there was probably not enough for her to join in. They never had the money for bus fares and walked or cycled everywhere. The children all had that practical, hard-working attitude instilled into them by their parents. Both sons went into the services, Jack right at the beginning of hostilities and Maurice joined the RAF when he was old enough. Sheila worked at AWA as a riveter and Eunice was a comptometer operator at AWA Whitley. She was also a member of the Women's Voluntary Service (WVS) and helped out serving drinks to bus drivers at a kiosk in Pool Meadow.

All three sisters loved dancing, it was the favourite entertainment of many in wartime and they were no exception. Rita was taught all the steps of the most popular dances by her sisters. It was common to see them dancing to the music on the wireless, moving through the house from the front room to the kitchen with a smooth rhythm, despite the confined space and the obstacle of furniture. Rita lived for Saturday night when she joined others at the Vecqueray Street youth club for dances. The crowd from the club went to the GEC ballroom for dances held there. Billy Monk and his band played there, entertaining the dancers with all the popular dance tunes. Rita always had to leave by 9pm and return home, as her dad was very strict. She always felt disappointed as the pace was just beginning to liven up and many were only just arriving. As she cycled home alone along Humber Avenue she was sorry to leave the noise and excitement of the dance.

When her sister Eunice was working at the WVS kiosk in Pool Meadow she got to know many of the firemen from the Fire Station nearby. The kiosk had no water and it had to be collected from the Fire Station. Rita, then fourteen, sometimes helped Eunice in the evening, until it closed around 9pm when the buses stopped running. The two girls were invited by the firemen to join them at one of their dances held in the Auxiliary Fire Service building on the corner of Ford Street and White Street. There was a beautiful dance floor upstairs and they had a dance band made up of members of the fire service. On the first occasion that Rita went she was very nervous, as there were many servicemen attending. When a soldier asked her to dance, she was very stiff as she was too nervous to relax and enjoy herself. As time went on she began to enjoy it and went several times with both of her sisters.

There were many other dance halls that the three sisters frequented, such as the Drill Hall on Saturday nights. Even pubs had small dance floors, as they catered for their customers' needs. Rita had a friend whose mother was a barmaid at the Charterhouse pub in Terry Road, where a small band with a few instruments played in the back room and the two friends went there on Friday night. Her favourite venue became the Rialto Casino in Coundon, where Johnny Pearson was the band leader. Rita often cycled or walked home from dances at midnight or 1.00am as she got older and never felt nervous.

When Rita began work on 4th January 1944 at Armstrong Siddeley, Parkside she hated it. The Dispatch Department, where she worked in the office, was situated in the area of the factory known as 'The Dump,' near London Road cemetery. All of the other female staff were older women working part-time, some doing mornings and some afternoons. She was supposed to leave at 5.30pm, but when none of the others began preparing to go she continued to work. The older women all did overtime to increase their wages and as her boss was out of the office, there was no one to ask. When he returned and found her still working, he was surprised and said she had to leave at 5.30pm because of her age, then only fourteen. Her wages for that first week came to seventeen shillings and sixpence because of the overtime she had done, but normally it was sixteen shillings and eight pence. She found the work of the Dispatch Dept. very interesting after the initial few weeks when she was very unhappy and nearly left. Her boss kept persuading her to stay a bit longer until she settled down and began to enjoy the job. The drivers used to take the engines made in the factory, all over the country on huge low-loaders, nicknamed Queen Mary's. Rita had to deal with their expenses, such as fuel at one shilling and nine pence per gallon and accommodation. Some went as far as Lossiemouth in Scotland and only recently she heard of a depot in Shropshire closing down, where engines were sent in the war. The thirty drivers made quite a fuss of Rita, being the only young woman in the department. She still has the card issued when she began work, with her shelter number, 15, stamped on it. It was a glorified name for a passageway between two of the factory buildings, with a roof over the top.

She stayed at Armstrong Siddeley for ten years until she married in 1954 and moved with her husband, Derek, to Radford. She found work very hard to obtain near to her home and worked briefly for Lustre Fibres, part of Courtaulds, before returning to Armstrong Siddeley for a further six and a half years until she began her family.

Strangely, when Rita and Derek were holidaying in Ibiza in the 1990s, they were sitting in the hotel reception when another couple came to sit by them. The man suddenly leaned across and said, 'I know you, you used to work at Siddeley.' He had worked in the pattern shop at The Dump when Rita used to sell National Savings stamps to the men. He said they always wondered why they saw her cycle up towards Parkside but never saw her return. She explained that she had to clock-in at Parkside, but not clock-out and went home in the opposite direction. What a small world it is! The two couples kept in touch and became good friends in the weeks that followed their return to Coventry and Bedworth, where the others lived. When Derek died suddenly soon afterwards, they proved a great support to Rita and her family.

Rita grew from a child to a working woman during the years of the war, but looks back on it with humour not dread. It disrupted family life when her brothers went into the forces and also her schooling due to the bombing, but they had many good times. They learned to live with the inconveniences of war and accept the disruption it brought. Life on the home front had to be made the best of, for there was no alternative.

Lynn Hockton

Interviewed August 2006

Muriel Sinclair

Muriel celebrated her 10th birthday on the 1st October 1939. Like many other children throughout the country, as soon as war had been declared, her parents arranged for her to be evacuated to the countryside, away from danger. She was more fortunate than a lot of children because she knew the people with whom she was to live.

Fred and Alice Baker lived in Claybrooke Magna, a small village in Leicestershire, a couple of miles off the A5 road. Fred was the village butcher who slaughtered his own animals for customers. He owned a van and extended his delivery service to the surrounding areas including Coventry. Muriel's mother had been a regular customer, for as long as she could remember, and over the years they became friends. As soon as war was declared Fred and his wife, Alice, offered to take Muriel to live with them. At the time they did not have any children of their own. Fred picked her up in his van one Sunday afternoon. It was the same van that he used for delivering his meat and there were some sheep in the back. She was made very welcome by Aunty Alice and was happy living with them. They treated her very well.

Initially Muriel only stayed with the Bakers for three weeks. As there had been no bombing in Coventry during that time her parents thought it safe for her to return home. Fred took her home when he delivered the meat to her mum. Many other children were also returned to the city when schools, which had been closed, were opened again. Muriel attended Frederick Bird School. Education was spasmodic, as many teachers were supporting the country in other ways, so staffing was a problem. They did have a few lessons in the school, but most were taken in various places and only for short periods. Two places she remembers were St Albans Church and a hut in Sackville Street, Hillfields.

Muriel's family home was in Nicholls Street, Hillfields, near Coventry City Football ground in Highfield Road. There were a lot of factories in the district and in the autumn of 1940 bombs were dropped in the area. At first it was not too bad, but when Clarke's Builders and Wood Yard, in Coronation Road, was bombed her dad decided it was time for her to go back to Claybrooke.

Her dad had an essential job at the Humber car factory and one of his colleagues owned a car so he took her back. This time an arrangement was made for Muriel's mum, dad, sister and brother-in-law to accompany her to Claybrooke each night. Fred Baker was to fetch them all and return them in the morning, for as long as he could get the petrol. A few weeks later

Muriel Sinclair

petrol was severely rationed. However, a neighbour in the village, who worked in Coventry and was allowed a petrol ration, took her family backwards and forwards when he travelled to work.

On the evening of the 14th November 1940 Muriel was taken to Nuneaton by the Bakers to stay with one of their friends, while Uncle Fred took Auntie Alice into Nuneaton hospital to have a baby. A boy was born during the night. He was named Roger and she will never forget his birthday. She is still good friends with him, his wife and daughter. After Fred picked her back up they came into Coventry to get her mum and dad. As they were going along Ansty Road the air raid sirens started. Fred put his foot down and they got back to Claybrooke in record time. As the evening and night progressed they went out and stood on the side of the road and watched Coventry burn, wondering what they would find next morning.

Muriel had to go back home with her family the following day, as there was no one to look after her at Claybrooke. Fred brought them back as far as he could, dodging the police who were stopping everyone entering the city. He managed to get them as far as the Craven Arms pub at the end of Binley Road, but they had to walk the rest of the way, which was rather scary. They passed bombed out houses some still burning, bomb craters, trams stranded in the middle of the road and people looking very shocked not knowing what to do. They wondered what they would find when they turned into Nicholls Street. The family were very lucky they had only had the windows blown out. Like everyone else they had no water, gas or electricity. Muriel's mum and dad transported water in large stone jars from Claybrooke, until they could get some at home. Muriel returned to the Baker's in Claybrooke.

It was a shock to her when she first started living in the country. There was no tap water in the house, nor a kitchen such as she had been used to. The pump was just outside the back door and she had to jump on the handle to get any water. Aunt Alice could work it with just one hand. The bucket toilet was emptied every week very early in the morning, although there were roses all around the entrance, which helped to mask any odour in the summer. It stood next to the washhouse, which housed a sink, without a tap, and a big 'copper.'

Muriel was the only evacuee from Coventry in the village, but there were a lot from London and they were very homesick. Some of them ran away and tried to get back home. They often did not get very far and were brought back. There was only one bus a week through the village, which ran from Hinckley to Lutterworth and there was a railway station at the next village, Ullesthorpe, with trains going to Rugby and Leicester. Some evacuees managed to get to London and stayed there. While some children had very nice homes and foster parents, others were not so lucky. Those living on farms had jobs to do. Muriel too, was expected to do some work. She used to deliver meat around the village, if the lad did not turn up, and always had to wash up and peel the potatoes at the weekends. However, there was plenty of time and space to play in the fields and around the farms.

During this period she attended the village school, which was small compared with Frederick Bird School. There were four classrooms, one for beginners, one for six to eight year olds and one for the older pupils. Another classroom was used as a dining room for the pupils who lived too far away to get home for dinner. The class she was in had three columns of desks, one for each of the years nine, ten and eleven. Another shock awaited her there as they gave her a slate and slate pencil; she had never seen one of these before. Pupils always had books and pencils at 'Freddy's.' Muriel remained there until September 1941 when all 11 year olds went to Lutterworth School.

A bus collected the children every morning and returned them after school. The bus did a school run before theirs, so they were last into school and first out. One day the children got tired of waiting for the bus and went to play in the local wood yard so did not see it come. Someone had to fetch them or they would have missed it. The winter of 1941 was a very bad one with heavy snowfalls so they could not go to school. For a day or two only the milk lorry managed to get through to collect milk from the farms.

Muriel remained in the village until April 1942. Her dad was not very well and they stayed at home over the weekend. The bombing had almost ceased. She cannot remember whether they had any more air raids, but her parents decided it was safe for her to return home permanently. She went back to Frederick Bird School in Swan Lane. Muriel had been ahead of the children in the village school, but was a little behind when she returned to her school in Coventry. Nevertheless, she soon settled back into town life at home with her parents.

For other than grammar school pupils it was customary to leave school at the age of fourteen. Muriel's fourteenth birthday coincided with an official leaving date, the October break in 1943, so she left on the Friday and began working at the Humber Car firm on the following Monday. She wanted to be an accounting machine operator like her sister, although the careers' advice staff did not seem to know anything about the work. As a junior employee, she had to work in various departments before she was allowed to work on the accounting machines. She had reached the age of seventeen before she became a National Accounting Machine Operator, the job she really wanted to do. She remained at the Humber until 1955.

During Muriel's leisure time she was a member of the Girl Guides until the age of fifteen, when she joined the British Red Cross Society. On Friday evenings she went to Keresley Hospital to help on the wards by giving out tea to the patients. She also attended Warwick Road Church and Youth Club.

In 1952 Muriel married Fred Sinclair with whom she had corresponded since they first met when she was fifteen. He was a regular soldier and appreciated her letters when stationed in Egypt.

Muriel has been back to Claybrooke several times since the end of the war. The Bakers went to live on a farm near Frolsworth for a while then moved to a farm at Dunchurch, near Rugby, which is still owned by the same family.

Christine Marsh

Thank you to Muriel for sharing her memories of the war years with us.

Childhood Memories

I was born in Coventry just after the war, as a child I well remember the many desolate sites, which were scattered throughout Coventry. I would play amongst the ruins of one of these sites at the top of the street in which I grew up. To locals it was known as the bombed buildings, although as a child I never associated the war with the piles of bricks and rubble where once houses would have stood. To me, it was just a great place to play and rummage through, looking for the many treasures that my friends and I would find amongst the debris.

Looking back it was probably a very dangerous place for children to play and would certainly be frowned upon today. The danger was not recognised by us and no matter how many times we were told not to play there, my brother and I always ended up at the bombed buildings, along with all the other kids in our street.

My mother once told me how a bomb had landed on the site and the blast shook the whole street, to such a degree, that when she came out of the air raid shelter she was expecting the whole street to be gone. Instead a row of houses at the top of the street had been totally blasted away and our house had been damaged.

As a child in the fifties I remember the city centre was like one big building site; cranes and bulldozers were everywhere. Some sites were being cleared and others were being knocked down. At the back of the old Empire cinema was another site full of rubble and bricks, where we children would play after coming out of the Saturday morning club, which was a picture house (cinema) special for children. It was not until I was a teenager queuing to go into the Empire cinema that I began to wonder about this site and what buildings had stood on it. It was then that I began to realise how much of our historic city was gone forever due to a war.

The war years could not have been easy for mothers, wives and children. The women not only had to contend with being parted from their husbands and children, as many were evacuated, but also with air raids, food shortages and management of the home.

During the Second World War my mother was left with four children whose ages ranged from five to ten. My father was in the Eighth Army, so was in the war from the beginning. The children were evacuated to the countryside only to be brought back to Coventry because they were treated so cruelly.

My sister Julia did not find it easy to speak of the time when she was evacuated to the village of Pailton, near Rugby. She was seven at the time,

Eileen was five, Stanley nine and Jimmy ten.They were placed with an elderly woman whose only companions had been a houseful of cats. Whilst she loved her pets, she had no time for children, and from the start made it quite clear, that she took them in under sufferance.

She was a cruel and cold woman; she did not help them to settle in and kept a big stick in a cupboard too high for any of them to reach. This was her disciplinary stick which she used much too often. She would threaten them, saying they would never see their mum again, if they told tales of how they were being treated. She also used her dark and musty cellar as a form of punishment. She would lock them in there, which terrified them, as all manner of creatures probably lived down there too.

Eileen and Julia were terrified of her and it was after she locked little Eileen in the cellar, (because she had started to wet the bed), and left her there all night, ignoring her crying and pleading to be let out, that Jimmy ran away and found his way back to Coventry. As soon as my mother knew what was happening she was on the first bus to Pailton. As soon as she arrived, she told the children to get their things together because they were leaving. The woman started to plead with my mother saying she could not manage without the allowance she was getting for taking the children into her home. My mother ignored her pleas and fetched them back to Coventry, where they stayed for the duration of the war.

My mother did not find it easy to feed and clothe four children on her army allowance, she had to make their clothes from any material she could get, sometimes cutting up old dresses that were too small and remaking them so that they would fit. Nothing was wasted, any old coats or dresses that were too far gone to do anything with, would be cut into strips to make rag rugs using sacking for the back and pulling the strips of fabric through with a peg hook. She also found it difficult to cope with all the family issues that occurred along the way. Leaking pipes in the winter, general house repairs and even changing plugs were all jobs she and many women were not used to contending with. Decorating the house was another job women found themselves with, paper was very precious and wallpaper was unobtainable. So my mother would emulsion her walls and stipple them with a sponge to make a pattern, as did many other people.

My father was given a short leave before returning abroad, a few weeks after he was gone my mother realised she was expecting another baby. It was nearly three years before my father returned home; my brother was over two years old, before he saw his daddy for the first time.

Gladys Marsh

My mother in-law, Gladys Marsh, was born in Coventry and was one of the eldest of nine children. When war broke out she was just eighteen years old. After leaving school she worked in a weaving factory for a short time before changing jobs, moving to Dickens the leather factory. It was here that she was working when war was declared, she was engaged to be married to Sid Marsh and they already had a date in mind for late in the year of 1940.

In the summer of 1939, Gladys went on her first holiday to the seaside. Being one of such a large family her parents had always struggled to manage day to day, so holidays had been the last thing on their minds. Gladys, Sid and friends of theirs, holidayed in Torquay, Devon. They had a wonderful time and before they left to come home, eagerly made arrangements with the landlady to return in the following summer of 1940. Little did they realise that war would be declared in the September of 1939 and affect all their ambitions for the following year.

Although people were given gas masks and instructions on how to use them, and many were issued with Anderson shelters for erection in their gardens as protection against air raids, it was still strenuously denied by the Prime Minister and government officials that war was imminent. Because of the careful preparation before war was declared, Gladys along with many others, was expecting bombs to come raining down on them from the moment war began. In reality this was far from the case, everything happened gradually. It was a few months later, that ration books were issued and then they began to notice a shortage in certain foods. Luxury goods such as exotic fruits from abroad were almost impossible to get hold of, in fact Gladys never had a banana all through the war.

Chocolate, sugar, coffee and tea, were all very scarce items and a real treat if obtained. Clothes were also rationed; an ordinary dress was about four coupons, whilst a long dress such as a wedding dress, was as much as eight coupons. The fashion was for shorter dresses with less material in them, due to the shortage of material in general. Silk stockings were like gold dust and women would dye their legs with boot polish, gravy browning or such like, drawing seams at the back of their legs with crayons to imitate the look of stockings.

During the early months of 1940 Sid and Gladys were still looking forward to going back to Torquay for their holidays and their wedding, which was to take place later in the year. So they were both bitterly disappointed when their plans had to be changed. Firstly they decided to postpone their wedding, because they intended to buy their own house, and were fearful of more bad raids, which had already damaged a lot of Coventry's properties. The second blow was the cancellation of their holiday, because it became impossible to determine how long a journey would take if an air raid occurred, as it affected all forms of transport and they were more frequent and intense around Coventry during the late Summer of 1940. When they were returning from a trip to Nottingham races, the train could only go as far as Nuneaton, because of air raids over Coventry. So Gladys, Sid and their friends had to walk home from Nuneaton to Coventry late at night. Gladys told me, 'The best form of transport at that time was a persons own two feet, so we spent our holidays that year going for walks in the nearby countryside'.

The first few air raids were quite frightening, occurring mainly when it was dark. The sirens went off about 10 or 15 minutes before an air raid began, which anticipated the danger. It sounded eerie in the dark, then the droning of the plane engines above would be heard. At first Gladys and her family would rush to their air raid shelter, but it was cold, damp and sometimes water logged, also the air raids were light and only lasted a few minutes. It was not long before they got used to the raids and began to ignore them preferring to stay in the warm until the all clear sounded.

When the air raids became more intense, Gladys had to change her job when the leather factory was bombed. For a short period she went to work for the Co-op but it was not long before that too was bombed and she ended up working in another factory. Sid was a machine operator, at Armstrong Siddeley and was classed as working in an essential job, so conscription into the army was deferred several times. After Armstrong Siddeley was bombed Sid went to work at British Thompson Houston (BTH).

Gladys remembers that an incendiary bomb landed in the fields at the back of Sid's mother's house in Wheelwright Lane. She recalls that all the neighbours were out with their buckets and spades digging the earth and throwing it over the flames to douse them. The Germans would use the fires as landmarks for bombing.

Dancing to live bands was a popular pastime for the young of this era. Sid and Gladys would occasionally go to Courtaulds' Club in Lockhurst Lane. No night was complete, however, before Gladys had danced the Lambeth walk which was her favourite dance. It was after one such night, when they were walking home that Gladys and Sid noticed the sky over Birmingham was blood red. They stood looking at it along with many other people, although no words were spoken. This was the night of Birmingham's worst bombing raid and it is etched on Gladys's memory to this day.

On the night of the Coventry blitz Sid, Gladys and her brother Charlie went to the Parkgate Pub for a drink. They had only just got their drinks and sat down when the warning sirens began. They quickly drank up, intending to rush home before the air raid started, but as they opened the pub door to leave, the bombs came raining down. The landlord invited his customers to go down into the cellar with the pub staff, rather than risking going home. Gladys, Sid and a few other customers took up his offer and quickly went into the cellar.

Charlie who loved a drink decided to stay upstairs in the bar with a few other fellows. After a while the bombs seemed to ease off a bit, one of the customers decided to go and get himself a drink. When he got back into the cellar, he said to the landlord, 'If you don't do something quickly you will have no ale left, they are drinking your bar dry up there.' The landlord replied 'Well they can carry on for I am not going up their until the all clear'. Meanwhile Charlie and the other fellows were happily helping themselves to the ale. By the time the bombing raid was over they were paralytic and could not stand up. Charlie had to crawl home that night and he always maintained that the Coventry blitz was the best night of his life.

Gladys had been waiting for a lull in the bombing so that she could go to the toilet, which was outside up a little pathway in the pub garden. Sid went with her and just as she was finished planes could be heard, Sid told her to hurry up and she ran down the path sorting her clothes out on the way. They had only just got back inside when a thud shook the cellar and they felt the floor move. When they went to go outside after the bombing had stopped, the door they had used was stuck fast. They all heaved against it, trying to force it open, but to no avail. So they climbed up the cellar stairs into the bar area.

The next day when Gladys was on her way to work, Parkgate Road was barricaded off, so she asked the warden in charge why the road was closed. He said 'There is an unexploded bomb at the back of the Parkgate Pub, blocking the cellar door'. If that bomb had exploded none of them would have lived to tell the tale.

In the summer of 1941 Gladys and Sid decided to go ahead with their wedding. Gladys decided to get married in a suit; it would have taken too many of her coupons to buy a wedding dress. Gladys's mother who was a widow at this time, (Gladys's dad had died when she was 15 years old) asked a close friend of the family, who was a baker, if he could make a wedding cake as a surprise for the couple. Dried fruit was hard to come by and most brides had sponge cakes, surrounded by a cardboard casing, made to look like icing sugar. Gladys was lucky their friend had enough fruit to make them a two tiered cake and also iced it. He asked her mother to keep it quiet in case other people complained when he could not do the same for them.

So it was in July 1941 Gladys became a war bride. She saved her coupons for food, which provided her and Sid's family with a buffet meal afterwards. They had only close family and a few friends as guests, although it was only a small wedding by today's standards it was quite fitting for the times. After borrowing the deposit money from Sid's mum, they brought their first home on Wheelwright Lane. It was a typical semi-detached three bedroomed house of the era and had a good- sized back garden.

At this time people were encouraged to grow their own vegetables. If they did not have a garden many people worked on allotments, which were scattered throughout the city. Gladys and Sid grew their own vegetables in the garden, potatoes, carrots, cabbages, beetroot and anything else they could grow. They also kept chickens at the bottom of the garden, and some people kept pigs, because nearly every kind of food was now hard to come by. Gladys would collect the eggs in the morning and put them into a water glass bucket, which contained isinglass, as a way of preserving eggs. She gave any spare to her mum and other members of their family. The one thing she would not do was pluck and draw the chickens that they ate, Sid had to do that.

During the war years people were encouraged to be thrifty 'make do and mend' was the ethos of the war years. Gladys along with many other women was a fine advocate of this. She knitted, mainly using wool from old pullovers and jumpers, which had to be unpicked and then rewound. She also made her own clothes, sometimes out of old garments, nothing was wasted. It was a time when people helped each other and exchanged goods if they could. People made their own preserves from home grown fruit or wild berries, such as blackberries and raspberries. It was second nature to their generation to help each other without any strings attached or gain for themselves, for everyone was in the same boat.

Gladys had her first baby in 1942, and their life had settled into a routine of sorts. It was in 1945 when the war was almost over that Sid was conscripted into the army. Gladys was expecting another baby so it was the last thing they wanted to happen. After Sid had completed six months training in Ireland, he came home in the July and with only a month's notice, was posted abroad for two years. Gladys was relieved when the Japanese war ended in August 1945 because they knew that after being in India for a short period Sid would be going to Malaya.

Money was not an issue because Gladys received an army allowance and also an allowance from BTH who were keeping Sid's job open for his return. Gladys was used to living on a small amount and so managed to make the money go round. She missed him though, and when her baby was born, Sid was away in India. Although they wrote to each other every day it would sometimes be weeks before she received any letters and then she would get a batch all in one go. Although the war had ended, for Gladys, family life did not return to normal until Sid returned home.

Christine Marsh

Interviewed November 2006.
Sadly Gladys died in July 2007

Irene

Irene became engaged on her birthday, September 9th 1940. At the time she was living with her parents in Foleshill. Many nights incendiaries were being dropped and their house had been hit, setting fire to their bedrooms. Firemen had put the fires out but the water had made the bedrooms uninhabitable. As a result of this they were all living in the rooms downstairs. The following day her fiancé had returned to his unit and that evening Irene took off her engagement ring and put it on the piano. A new coat and hat were hanging on the picture rail. Darkness came bringing with it another raid. The road outside was a sea of burning incendiaries. Police were knocking on the door telling them to get out and go to the shelter. Fine; but how were they supposed to cross the road? A gallant policeman came to Irene's rescue and carried her across. It was at this moment that she remembered her engagement ring was still on the piano and her new coat and hat still on the picture rail. Her immediate impulse was to go back for them but the arm of the law, very firmly, said no. After much pleading the wonderful policeman said he would go back and fetch them for her. Such kindness. On the way back to his unit, the train that her fiancé was travelling in was held up; and from the train he watched a ferocious battle taking place in the skies overhead. It was a part of what came to be known as the Battle of Britain.

The next day, like everyone else, Irene went to work. She was employed, by a firm in Foleshill, as a shorthand typist. As this was not a 'reserved occupation' she had signed up to go into the Women's Auxiliary Air Force, her fiancé being in the Royal Air Force. He had come to Coventry before the war started and decided to buy a house with the intention of bringing his parents to live in Coventry as well. In due time this was what they had done. However, war came and he volunteered for the RAF, but because his eyesight was poor he was allocated to clerical work. On the day he left to join up his mother prepared a big tea for all the family, but no one had any appetite. After several weeks of training he came home on leave, but Irene recalls, he was a changed man.

September and October passed and it was now November. November 14th 1940, a date to remember. Because their home, in Cross Road, was in such close proximity to Alfred Herbert's machine tools factory, raids were a regular occurrence. After three successive nights of incendiary bombs and near misses, Irene and her mother decided to spend the night with her fiance's parents in Elgar Road – a much safer place – or so they thought. Her father stayed behind as he was on fire-watching duty. After a quick meal they set off, but by the time they had reached the Morris factory gates on Bell Green

Road the enemy aircraft were overhead. As they approached Elgar Road they could see the skies above the city centre, red from the reflection of the burning fires. They had only just got into the house when a bomb exploded nearby. Soot came down the chimney, pictures and ornaments fell, windows and doors blew in and almost immediately there was a banging on the door and a voice telling them to get out. An unexploded landmine had fallen just beyond the back gate. Everyone grabbed a bag, threw some things into it and made for the door. Irene's future mother-in-law threw more things in as they went by. When they reached the brick built air raid shelter on the pavement of Purcell Road everyone stopped and took cover. They had barely been in the shelter more than a few minutes when the Air Raid Warden shouted that he could hear ticking. Consternation, where was the bomb? Eventually it was discovered that the ticking was coming from Irene's bag! In her haste, her mother-in-law had pushed the alarm clock into it. Irene remembers the dreadful noise, continuous bombing, the bitterly cold moonlit night, and the horror of it all. The next morning when they came out of the shelter they had nowhere to go, houses were still on fire, unexploded bombs, no water, gas or electricity. But in nearby Sullivan Road a lady, who had one room still intact, invited them all in. Nine of them managed to get a little sleep on this kind lady's dining room floor. She was even able to find a little food from somewhere. Gradually news filtered through that Cross Road was badly hit. The chances of her father being alive seemed pretty slim. After a while Irene traced her steps back home. On entering the house there was her father standing in the kitchen, trying to pick all the bits out of a tin of condensed milk. He was endeavouring to make a 'mashing' of cocoa and milk to take with him to work. When asked how he had survived the night, his reply was 'It was a bit noisy.' This from a man who was a little hard of hearing!

Wedding plans were made for June 1941 and as her fiancé was away her future brother-in-law helped Irene to make all the arrangements. He went with her to buy the ring from James Walker the jewellers. The Geisha Café was booked for the reception and a wedding cake was ordered.

Her brother-in-law to be was a pharmaceutical chemist in Coventry but, unfortunately, he was severely asthmatic. Despite this he volunteered as an Air Raid Warden.

April 9th 1941, the night of another big raid. After a while everything went quiet and it seemed that the raid was over. The 'All Clear' had not been sounded but because it was so quiet people started to emerge from the shelter, including Irene. She was sitting on a wall when the next wave of enemy aircraft came over, and as she sat, she watched as the Daimler factory was bombed. In another part of town her brother-in-law was on ARP duty.

The first wave of the raid being over he popped home, with his neighbour, for a cup of coffee. Refreshed they started to walk back across the road just as the second wave of aircraft started dropping their bombs. Quickly they took cover under a vehicle on the opposite side of the road. A bomb dropped at the side of the vehicle and Irene's brother-in-law took the full blast. He was killed instantly. Two others, who were with him, were protected by the wheel of the lorry. His friends carried him into his house. There they removed the coalhouse door and laid him on it and then put him on the floor of his front room. Many were killed that night. Because of the situation the authorities decided that all the casualties would be buried in a mass grave and so men were dispatched all over the city to collect the bodies. They came knocking on the door but Irene's sister would not let them in. She did not want her husband to be put in a mass grave, she wanted to bury him in the graveyard of their local church. After some days the police were sent to collect the body. Knowing they were coming, the front room was locked; Irene took the keys, put them in her pocket and went into town.... It was a big funeral. Many of his colleagues and friends lined the route and he was laid to rest in the graveyard of his local church.

Irene's immediate reaction was to cancel her wedding plans but her sister insisted that they went ahead. She said they were all going to wear their nice clothes come what may. But one of Irene's memories of her big day is hearing her sister quietly sobbing as she walked down the aisle.

Her sister was now on her own, so her mother and father decided to give up their home and, together with Irene, go and live with their daughter.

Life went on. Irene had now been made assistant company secretary where she worked, so this meant she was now in a 'reserved occupation' and not required to go into the Forces. Leaving for work each day she would say 'cheerio' to her mother, both of them not knowing if they would see one another again. Death was ever present and everyone lived with this shadow hanging over them.

The day of the wedding was approaching. Both Irene and her fiancé were Sunday School teachers at Saint Paul's Church, Foleshill and, naturally enough, it was there that they wanted to be married. But it was not to be. Their Banns had already been read once when fate intervened. The church was bombed and Irene cried as she watched the church doors fall off. Just another little hitch. However, the vicar of St. Paul's came to the rescue. He contacted the vicar of Holy Trinity Church and asked him if they could use his church instead. He readily agreed. Even then, when it came to the blessing, they were not able to walk up the aisle as there was a big hole in the Chancel floor. Instead the blessing was given in the Nave. The wedding cake was a chocoholics dream. It was three-tiered and each tier was covered in chocolate (icing sugar not being available). Thick chocolate baskets decorated the sides of the cakes and in each basket there was orange blossom. On the top were two intertwined rings with a dove standing on them. A creation indeed. It was the custom to keep one of the tiers for future use as a Christening cake but to Irene's dismay, she found on her return from honeymoon, that the wedding guests had eaten all the chocolate!

The honeymoon was to be taken in South Wales where her husband had friends. They had been invited to stay for a week. First they missed the train from Coventry, so they had to go by a different route. This required a stop in Malvern. Her new husband went off to find something to eat and drink. All he could find was one Bovril sandwich and no drink. He brought it back to Irene and asked, 'Are you going to share it?' The look on her face gave him his answer. So, waste not, want not, he ate it. Next they had to catch another train to get them to Newport but even this was not uneventful. A raid caused the train to wait in a tunnel and so it was the early hours of the morning before they finally arrived at their destination. On alighting from the train there were, of course, no lights on. Their friends had left, thinking they were not coming, so they had nowhere to go. Two people on an empty station, not knowing what to do, found themselves confronted by a policeman. 'Aye, aye, what are you doing? - Come with me.' He guided them through the streets until they reached a hotel where he hammered on the door. Thankfully they were able to spend what was left of their wedding night in the warm. Later that day they were able to find their friends but fate still continued to intervene. On the news the next night it was announced that the hotel where they had stayed the previous night had been bombed. For a treat they decided to go to Barry Island for the day. But even here there was no escape. An enemy aircraft came flying over firing his guns. Both of them flung themselves onto the ground and remained completely still until the plane had flown by.

The year turned and 1941 became 1942 and Irene found that she was pregnant. She continued to work. Ironically, the authorities still thought that she was liable for call-up and she was actually called before a board to prove that she was pregnant.

One night, when the air raid warning sounded, her mother and sister took off for the shelter. For some reason Irene was not ready and by the time she set off the raid was well and truly underway. A passing fireman made her lie down on the ground and he flung himself on top of her to protect her. There they stayed until the raid was over. Such a brave act from a complete stranger.

The baby was due in August, and like many other expectant mothers, when her due date arrived Irene was evacuated out of Coventry. It was not a pleasant time. The baby decided to wait another two weeks before it arrived. Whilst there, Irene was instructed to take up a long carpet runner from the landing, take it downstairs, beat it and then return it upstairs. When her husband learned of the imminent birth of the baby he sent a telegram to her. However, the telegram was not given to Irene personally but pinned up on a notice board for everyone to see. Irene was in bed when her waters broke. She now had to be transferred to the main hospital. A taxi was called. On its arrival, Irene was expected to wait while the taxi driver was made a cup of tea and while he drank it. She was then expected to bring down her own case and carry it to the taxi. A less than happy experience, but finally Irene gave birth to a healthy baby girl.

Irene's husband was posted all over Britain at different times, but if he was able to rent a room nearby for a day or two it meant that she and the baby could go and see him. Filey was one of his postings and finding a room he asked Irene and the baby to come. The little one was still small so she had to travel in her pram. So taking pram, luggage and herself was a considerable undertaking. Her mother was quite convinced that she would not make it, but went with her as far as Birmingham. It took five changes of train to get to Filey. All the trains were packed with soldiers so there was no shortage of helping hands to speed her on her way. The day after her arrival Irene took the baby to see her Daddy march through the streets of Filey. He had been posted again. So after just one day, Irene had to make her way back home. Another posting was to Cambridgeshire. Again, he was able to find a room, and this time the accommodation was on the edge of the airfield. Their time together however, was brief. A despatch rider arrived to call him back to the base. From the bedroom window Irene watched as wave after wave of bombers took to the skies. She did not know what was happening - was it a big raid, or was it invasion? The date was June 6th 1944, D-day.

Life went on, people adapted and made the best of things. Each Friday Irene would walk into town, with the baby in her pram, to do the shopping. It was considered a rare treat if she came home with some broken biscuits from the shop at the bottom of the Arcade.

One Christmas, despite the lack of conventional ingredients, Irene and her sister decided to make a cake. They used dried egg and whatever else they could find that they thought might make a recognizable cake. It turned into quite a large mixture. It was put in the oven to bake but each time they tested it the bit in the middle stubbornly remained uncooked. This happened more than once, by which time the outside of the cake was getting a bit burnt. So, undeterred, they started cutting the burnt bits off. In the end they stayed up all night, testing the cake, cutting burnt bits off, until finally, what was left was a rather small offering. The final insult being that it did not taste very nice either!

On another occasion, when her mother was making a cake, she mistakenly used her husband's stomach powder instead of flour. However, he ate the cake. Well, it was a novel way of taking his medicine! In those days there was always a good amount of cream on the top of the milk. Each day this was saved, and at the end of the week one of the family would sit and shake it until it separated out. It was then washed under the tap, a little salt added; the result being a small amount of delicious butter. At Easter time the baby never went without an Easter egg. Irene would blow a hen's egg and then fill it with chocolate. The chocolate came from her husband and his Air Force friends.

After her brother-in-law's death her sister went to work on the buses. Here she was to meet a man whose fiancée had also been killed. Their shared experiences brought them together and soon they were married. So Irene found her life very full and busy.

Her father-in-law had suffered a stroke and he and his wife were advised to move out of Coventry. The house that her husband had bought was now left empty. Accommodation, of course, was at a premium, so the house had to be rented out and a married couple moved in. But, as time went by, Irene longed for a home of her own. The war was now coming to an end so it was decided to ask the couple if they were prepared to move out. They refused and continued to do so until, eventually, the case had to go to court. On the second occasion in court, the occupier conceded he was willing to share the house. Irene could have the front rooms but to use the kitchen and the toilet she would have to go round the outside of the house, as she would not be allowed to walk through his rooms. The judge immediately ruled in Irene's favour and gave the couple a month to move out. Sadly, the man caused a lot of damage to the house before he left.

The war came to an end and Irene and her husband settled down to family life. It had been an extremely eventful time for her but most of her memories are happy ones. Despite the ups and downs it is the memories of people's kindness that have stayed with her.

June Hill

My thanks go to Irene for talking to me. The time passed so quickly in her most interesting company.
August 2007.

Reminiscences over Coffee

The following five pieces were the result of a pleasant chat over coffee.

Irene Cole (nee Allsopp)

Irene was born in Earlsdon in 1924; grew up in Melbourne Road; went to Centaur Road School; and in 1938, at fourteen years of age, entered the world of work. She went to earn her living at the Coventry Gauge and Tool Company, a large machine tool manufacturer. Her employers sent her to a school in Birmingham where she was trained to be a Comptometer Operator. Back at the Gauge and Tool, Irene worked from 8.30a.m till 5.30p.m each day, in the Wages Department. Sometimes it was necessary to work Monday evenings in preparation for the wages payout on Thursday. One year the girls even had to work on Christmas Day.

Irene was a typical teenager with a great love of dancing. Along with a group of girls, she would go dancing in the ballroom at the bottom of Broomfield Road. Another favourite was the cinema, and Earlsdon certainly had plenty of these. With films changed regularly it was possible to see three different films in a week. As the cinema was such a popular pastime it is not surprising that this is where Irene met her future husband.

As with most people at this time, the bicycle was the main form of transport, and Irene went everywhere on her bike, including to and from work. Stratford-upon-Avon is approximately twenty miles away from Coventry but most weekends the girls would cycle over there, go boating on the river, have a drink in the pub and then cycle all the way back again. Great exercise, but perhaps the attraction was the number of Americans and Canadians to be found in Stratford at this time!

On one occasion, cycling to Stratford, the girls were riding three abreast down Stoneleigh Hill. They were all so busy talking, that their handlebars locked; and over the handlebars went the girls, onto the road. A lorry driver coming in the opposite direction stopped to pick them up and all three of them came home on the back of the lorry together with their mangled bicycles.

Life would appear to have been quite normal – but, of course, it was not.

After the November 1940 blitz, when Irene got home from work, her father took her down the town to see what the bombs had done. They walked into town and both of them were shocked to see the damage that had been caused.

Irene and Harry Cole

In the streets of terraced houses there was a great sense of community. When the bombs were dropping neighbours would congregate together. Irene, however, never went down the shelter. When the alarm went off her boyfriend would come round and they would shelter under the wooden dining table. But, in 1941, at nineteen years of age, her boyfriend, Harry, was called up and he chose to go into the Navy, to serve on H.M.S. Frobisher.

At the beginning of April 1944, Irene received a telegram from Harry telling her to get ready as they were going to be married. With four days notice Irene had to do everything. She arranged the service, borrowed a dress, booked Taylers to take the photographs and on April 8th, Irene and Harry were wed. Fortunately they were able to have two days honeymoon in Stratford before Harry had to return to his ship.

After marriage Irene moved to Craven Street, where she lived with her Aunt. She wrote many letters to her husband during his time away, and he to her.

In Craven Street there is a public house called The Hearsall Inn and Irene recalls that the customers who were away in the Forces were not forgotten. Letters were written to them and sometimes money was sent as well.

Happily, Harry returned and was 'demobbed' in 1945 to resume his pre-war job as a capstan operator at the Standard Motor Company.

Joan Dean (nee Kettle)

Joan was fifteen when the war started. She was one of two girls and the family lived in Brays Lane, Stoke.

Joan was employed at Patrick's Department Store, which at this time, was in Much Park Street. She worked in the millinery department making hats and also curtains. Each day she would walk into work and her week's wages were twelve shillings and six pence. Patrick's Department Store was one of the casualties of the Blitz. It had been a very tall building but it was bombed right down to the cellars. Joan went into town the next day with her mother to see the damage. Patrick's quickly relocated to Trinity Street where they were one of a very few shops to open.

Everything was on coupons during the war but grey blankets were available to buy. Being an excellent seamstress, Joan was able to make herself a coat from one of these.

Joan's great passion was dancing. She used to go two or three times a week to Pattison's dancing school, where she had lessons. Using her creative skills, she made her skirts for dancing out of parachute material. It was at the dancing club that she met her future husband.

Joan and Frank Dean's Wedding

There were many shortages but people managed and found alternatives. Joan remembers making custard with ordinary flour and a bright yellow liquid, which you could buy in a bottle. It was hard to mix and did not taste very nice either. Instead of fresh eggs, dried eggs were used, and the one thing she hated was Spam!

Joan's boyfriend, Frank, worked for the Alvis Company, but the factory became another casualty of war. A direct hit on the tool room meant all production was lost. Plans were made to move the tool room workers to a small factory in the village of Anstey in Leicestershire and brick built prefabricated bungalows were built to house them. Frank was allocated one of these bungalows so they brought forward their marriage plans so that they could take up the offer.

Everything, of course, was on coupons but the family rallied round. Her grandfather gave her coupons, her sister made her wedding dress and Joan, herself, made the bridesmaids dresses. There were four of them, one blue, one pink, one yellow and one green. She was married at St. Michael's church, Stoke and afterwards a reception was held in her mother's house. The happy pair were able to have a wedding cake, but not a honeymoon.

Furniture, like everything else, was on coupons, but they were able to get utility furniture to furnish their new home. She did not mind the move away from her family but regularly went back to see them, travelling on the bus. Whilst there, Joan worked for the British Thompson - Houston Company (B.T.H.) in Leicester on radar and inspection.

Much later, when the war with Germany was over but the war with Japan was still ongoing, Frank was conscripted into the Army. Those men who had been in 'reserved occupations' had to do a two-year stint. Frank went into the Pay Corps and was given a Civilian posting in Manchester. This meant that Joan was able to join him. First of all Joan got a job in a biscuit factory and then she went to work for Lewis' Department Store. She recalls her time here as very pleasant. There were many dance halls, cinemas and parks – plenty of life. Frank was able to enjoy the football. It was also easy to get reasonably priced meat so, although their accommodation was not quite to their liking, life was good and they were tempted to stay. But they both decided that they wanted to be near their families so Joan returned to Coventry and went to live with her mother.

Her abilities as a needlewoman, again, proved most useful. She was able to sew for both herself and her mum. She would also knit when she was able to get the wool.

Wartime brought many shortages but people were most inventive and always found alternatives. Joan, like so many others, used her skills to great effect for the benefit of herself and those around her.

Betty Eccles (nee Brookfield)

Betty Eccles and her Sister

Betty was living in Wem, Shropshire when her husband found he was to work for Wickman Machine Tools in Coventry. So, with her husband and small family, Betty came to live in Coventry.

Shortly after this move, her husband was drafted into the Forces and he became a Despatch Rider in the Middle East.

Betty recalls, vividly, the day that he returned home from the war. Her daughter Pam, aged seven, was already in bed, but on hearing her father at the door, she hurtled down the stairs. Betty's baby son, who was finishing his tea at the time, promptly put the remains of his pudding on his head. A treasured memory, which Betty still remembers with a smile and a giggle.

Rene Frost (nee Tedds) and Joyce Cole (nee Frost)

Rene was born in Longford in 1913. By the age of three she was going to the nursery school just down the road from where she lived and following this she went to Longford School which was just across the road from where she lived. So her mother was able to bring her a cup of cocoa at break times. All of this whilst the First World War was raging across the Channel.

Rene's grandmother did the washing for a Doctor Webster and his household, so as a youngster she was sometimes allowed to go up to the big house. At Christmas time, just after the First World War had ended, she was again allowed to go up to the big house to see the Christmas tree, which, she recalls, went from floor to ceiling.

By the time the Second World War came Rene was married with a family of her own. Her husband was working for Webster and Bennett as a machine tool fitter.

Rene epitomizes a member of a big family unit, all members living quite close to one another, helping each other out when the occasion required it. Rene was the only girl in her family, with four brothers, so the responsibility of care fell onto her shoulders. Her mother had a job as a cleaner in a school but she also looked after her own brother, Jack, who lived with her, but had TB. So when she was poorly it was Rene who went and did her housework for her. There was her husband's family to care for too.

Living close by was a Mrs. Jackson, a lady certainly in her eighties. Rene kept an eye on her as well, to make sure she was all right, as she did not have any family of her own. Mrs. Jackson was a strong-minded old lady who refused to go down the shelter when the sirens sounded. Even the local doctor could not persuade her to take cover. He knocked on Rene's door and told her to leave and take her family down the shelter. The one that they used was situated under Foleshill Bridge. There were benches inside but you had to go down early if you wanted to get a seat. After a raid, when they came up out of the shelter, they always went to see if Mrs. Jackson was all right. But on this occasion she was not there. She had gone. A niece from Fillongley had come and taken her away. She never returned.

The day came when Rene's house was bombed and off the family went to live in Boston Place, Foleshill. Boston Place was an old court with dwellings on all sides. In the washhouse there was one copper boiler for five families. Rene was second in line. Monday was wash day. The copper was boiled and the first lady would do her washing. When she had finished she would tell Rene who could then do her washing. When Rene was finished she would tell the next one in line. And so on. Joyce clearly remembers the big old mangle that everyone used.

A lady called Ada Watts kept the shop on the corner of the court. There you were able to get things on a daily basis and at the end of the week you paid your bill. Once a week you did a shop at the Co – op.

Routine was of great importance in those days. Washing on Monday, ironing on Wednesday, baking on Thursday, black lead the grates on Friday. Friday was also the day to scrub grandmother's floor. Rene was only allowed to scrub four tiles at a time and grandmother stood over her to make sure that she did the job properly. It was a big floor! Saturday they all went to see Rene's mother at Longford, all together for a family tea. They would go over on the tram but walk back. Sunday was the day that they visited her husband's family. Amidst all this daily routine the enemy struck again. A bomb dropped into the middle of the court. Fortunately no one was killed as they were all down the shelter.

Joyce recalls another time when they were down the shelter, the warden arrived and told them all to get out and find another place to take cover. They thought a gas bomb had been dropped. At the time she was only seven years old but she can still remember the words of the warden 'Sing you buggars, sing and get out.'

The family was eventually to settle in Rollason Road.

Families together – where women most certainly played their part.

Joan Morgan

Joan seems to have been a bit of a rebel. In 1937 she had gone to work in a big house as a nursemaid to two little girls aged two and a half years and six months. She lived in, and for her work she was paid thirty shillings a month. Her own home was ten miles away. So every month, Joan would cycle home to give the thirty shillings to her mother. Her mother would then give her twenty pence back for herself. Joan did not have much spare time looking after two small children and also helping to prepare breakfast each day. When asked if she would help with the washing as well, Joan rebelled and said no.

In 1942 Joan went to work for the Standard Motor Company, Aero Division, where she worked on a soldering machine. Many girls came from London to work there. Not long after joining the Standard workforce, Joan along with the girls from London, was told to go to Rugby where they were all to work on the buses. Joan again rebelled and said no. Because the jobs that they were doing were not 'reserved occupations' the girls were expected to go where they were told to go. Joan was threatened with a five pound fine or imprisonment. This was no contest so in the end she agreed.

All the girls were given money to pay for a hostel but Joan did not like this so she found herself alternative lodgings. This meant a bus journey into Rugby each day. Joan worked on long distance runs to Lutterworth and Daventry picking up workmen to take them into work.

On the day war ended Joan was in bed when the news came through. Rebel to the end, she immediately gave in her notice.

June Hill

111

My thanks are due to Irene, Pam, Joan, Betty, Rene, Joyce and Joan for sharing their reminiscences with me. It was a privilege to be in their company and the coffee was nice too.
August 2007.

V.E. Party, Newey Road , Wyken, Coventry   Kind Permission of Vic Terry